HowExpe

How to Tr
Mountains in Nepal

A Quick and Comprehensive Guide to Trekking the Manaslu Mountains of Nepal from A to Z

HowExpert with Rebecca Friedberg

Copyright HowExpert™
www.HowExpert.com

For more tips related to this topic, visit HowExpert.com/manaslu.

Recommended Resources

- HowExpert.com – Quick 'How To' Guides on All Topics from A to Z by Everyday Experts.
- HowExpert.com/free – Free HowExpert Email Newsletter.
- HowExpert.com/books – HowExpert Books
- HowExpert.com/courses – HowExpert Courses
- HowExpert.com/clothing – HowExpert Clothing
- HowExpert.com/membership – HowExpert Membership Site
- HowExpert.com/affiliates – HowExpert Affiliate Program
- HowExpert.com/writers – Write About Your #1 Passion/Knowledge/Expertise & Become a HowExpert Author.
- HowExpert.com/resources – Additional HowExpert Recommended Resources
- YouTube.com/HowExpert – Subscribe to HowExpert YouTube.
- Instagram.com/HowExpert – Follow HowExpert on Instagram.
- Facebook.com/HowExpert – Follow HowExpert on Facebook.

COPYRIGHT, LEGAL NOTICE AND DISCLAIMER:

COPYRIGHT © BY HOWEXPERT™ (OWNED BY HOT METHODS). ALL RIGHTS RESERVED WORLDWIDE. NO PART OF THIS PUBLICATION MAY BE REPRODUCED IN ANY FORM OR BY ANY MEANS, INCLUDING SCANNING, PHOTOCOPYING, OR OTHERWISE WITHOUT PRIOR WRITTEN PERMISSION OF THE COPYRIGHT HOLDER.

DISCLAIMER AND TERMS OF USE: PLEASE NOTE THAT MUCH OF THIS PUBLICATION IS BASED ON PERSONAL EXPERIENCE AND ANECDOTAL EVIDENCE. ALTHOUGH THE AUTHOR AND PUBLISHER HAVE MADE EVERY REASONABLE ATTEMPT TO ACHIEVE COMPLETE ACCURACY OF THE CONTENT IN THIS GUIDE, THEY ASSUME NO RESPONSIBILITY FOR ERRORS OR OMISSIONS. ALSO, YOU SHOULD USE THIS INFORMATION AS YOU SEE FIT, AND AT YOUR OWN RISK. YOUR PARTICULAR SITUATION MAY NOT BE EXACTLY SUITED TO THE EXAMPLES ILLUSTRATED HERE; IN FACT, IT'S LIKELY THAT THEY WON'T BE THE SAME, AND YOU SHOULD ADJUST YOUR USE OF THE INFORMATION AND RECOMMENDATIONS ACCORDINGLY.

THE AUTHOR AND PUBLISHER DO NOT WARRANT THE PERFORMANCE, EFFECTIVENESS OR APPLICABILITY OF ANY SITES LISTED OR LINKED TO IN THIS BOOK. ALL LINKS ARE FOR INFORMATION PURPOSES ONLY AND ARE NOT WARRANTED FOR CONTENT, ACCURACY OR ANY OTHER IMPLIED OR EXPLICIT PURPOSE.

ANY TRADEMARKS, SERVICE MARKS, PRODUCT NAMES OR NAMED FEATURES ARE ASSUMED TO BE THE PROPERTY OF THEIR RESPECTIVE OWNERS, AND ARE USED ONLY FOR REFERENCE. THERE IS NO IMPLIED ENDORSEMENT IF WE USE ONE OF THESE TERMS.

NO PART OF THIS BOOK MAY BE REPRODUCED, STORED IN A RETRIEVAL SYSTEM, OR TRANSMITTED BY ANY OTHER MEANS: ELECTRONIC, MECHANICAL, PHOTOCOPYING, RECORDING, OR OTHERWISE, WITHOUT THE PRIOR WRITTEN PERMISSION OF THE AUTHOR.

ANY VIOLATION BY STEALING THIS BOOK OR DOWNLOADING OR SHARING IT ILLEGALLY WILL BE PROSECUTED BY LAWYERS TO THE FULLEST EXTENT. THIS PUBLICATION IS PROTECTED UNDER THE US COPYRIGHT ACT OF 1976 AND ALL OTHER APPLICABLE INTERNATIONAL, FEDERAL, STATE AND LOCAL LAWS AND ALL RIGHTS ARE RESERVED, INCLUDING RESALE RIGHTS: YOU ARE NOT ALLOWED TO GIVE OR SELL THIS GUIDE TO ANYONE ELSE.

THIS PUBLICATION IS DESIGNED TO PROVIDE ACCURATE AND AUTHORITATIVE INFORMATION WITH REGARD TO THE SUBJECT MATTER COVERED. IT IS SOLD WITH THE UNDERSTANDING THAT THE AUTHORS AND PUBLISHERS ARE NOT ENGAGED IN RENDERING LEGAL, FINANCIAL, OR OTHER PROFESSIONAL ADVICE. LAWS AND PRACTICES OFTEN VARY FROM STATE TO STATE AND IF LEGAL OR OTHER EXPERT ASSISTANCE IS REQUIRED, THE SERVICES OF A PROFESSIONAL SHOULD BE SOUGHT. THE AUTHORS AND PUBLISHER SPECIFICALLY DISCLAIM ANY LIABILITY THAT IS INCURRED FROM THE USE OR APPLICATION OF THE CONTENTS OF THIS BOOK.

COPYRIGHT BY HOWEXPERT™ (OWNED BY HOT METHODS) ALL RIGHTS RESERVED WORLDWIDE.

Table of Contents

Recommended Resources 2

Introduction..7

Chapter 1: How to Choose Mountain to Trek: Why Manaslu 9

When to Go Trekking 9

Other Treks 12

    Kangchenjunga Trek..12

    Upper Mustang Trek 13

    Three Passes Trek...13

    Dhaulagiri Circuit Trek.....................................14

    Annapurna Dhaulagiri Trek 15

    Annapurna Circuit Trek 16

    Rara Lake Trek 16

    Annapurna Base Camp Trek...............................17

    Makalu Base Camp Trek 18

    Upper Dolpo Trek...18

    Langtang Valley Trek...19

Why Trek Manaslu 20

Trek Lengths...23

Trekking Difficulty Grades 24

    Easy Trek Grades..25

    Moderate Trek Grades 26

    Challenging or Strenuous Trek Grades 26

    Very Challenging or Strenuous Trek Grade.........27

Chapter 2: Independent or Guided Trekking 29

Independent Trekking..29

    Preparing for an Independent Trek....................30

    Independent Trekking Pros................................31

    Independent Trekking Cons 32

Guided Trekking...34

    Guided Trekking Pros 35

    Guided Trekking Cons 36

Selecting a Trekking Agency 38

    Five Factors to Look for in Every Trekking Agency 38

    Eight Steps to Choose the Best Trekking Agency...............40

Porters and Guides...42

    How to Choose a Guide.....................................44

    What to Know When Trekking with a Guide......................45

How to Find Trekking Companions *46*
Finding Your Trekking Companion 47

Chapter 3: How to Prepare for Manaslu 50
What Gear to Buy *51*
Suggested Gear List for Tea House Trekking.....................51
Where to Buy the Gear *57*
Shopping in Kathmandu..58
Renting Reliable Trekking Gear...59
Purchasing from Brand Names 60
Visa Lengths and Fees *61*
Obtaining a Visa through a Consulate 62
Obtaining a Visa Upon Arrival...63
Visa Upon Arrival Overland...64
Visa Upon Arrival at the Airport..64
Park and Permit Fees...*66*
Trekking Permits..66
Permits and Park Entrance Fees for the Manaslu Trek 69
Arranging Transportation *70*
Local Bus 70
Tourist Bus...71
Private Jeep 72
Overall, I'm glad I took the local bus for my first time
trekking in Nepal. However, if I go trekking again, I
would pay the extra money to take a tourist bus or find
enough trekking companions to hire a private jeep..........73
Storing Your Luggage...*73*

Chapter 4: What to Expect on the Trek 75
Overview of Manaslu *76*
Sample Manaslu Trek Itinerary 76
Daily Routine..*79*
A Typical Day on a Trek 79
On the Trails...*80*
At the Tea Houses *81*
Tea House Facilities 82
Spending Time at the Tea Houses 83
Food and Water *84*
Water 84
Food...84
Experiencing Nepali Culture *85*
Common Courtesies...86
Eating 87
Temples 87

5

Meeting the Locals 88
Photo Taking 89

Chapter 5: Bumps on the Trails 90

General Safety Tips...*90*

Altitude Sickness and Diarrhea *91*

Altitude Sickness 92
Preventing Altitude Sickness 94
Diarrhea 96

Staying Motivated *98*

Surround Yourself with People 99
Make and Accept Mistakes 99
Think About the Big Picture 99
Take Pictures 100

Chapter 6: Trekking Manaslu: A Day-by-Day Account...101

Day 1 ....*102*
Day 2...*103*
Day 3...*105*
Day 4...*106*
Day 5 ....*107*
Day 6...*108*
Day 7...*109*
Day 8 ....*111*
Day 9 ....*112*
Day 10...*113*
Day 11 ....*114*
Day 12...*115*
Day 13 ....*116*
Day 14 ....*120*
Day 15 ....*121*
Day 16 ....*122*

Chapter 7: End of Trek 123

Tipping Your Guide and Porter *123*

Saying Good-Bye and Keeping in Touch............................*123*

Takeaway and Lessons Learned *124*

About the Expert.......................................126

Recommended Resources 127

Introduction

If you're traveling to Nepal, you're probably planning to trek through one of the Nepali mountains.

Why wouldn't you?

Nepal is home to some of the most impressive and breath-taking mountains in the world. It's where you can have a unique and eye-opening experience.

The Nepali mountains are the only place you can find sky-reaching mountain peaks, Buddhist monks meditating in mountainside monasteries, and teams of donkeys carrying goods to the nearest village.

It's a once-in-a-lifetime experience you don't want to pass up.

Before you even begin your trek, you might ask: Which mountain do I choose to trek? How long do I want to be in the mountains? What gear do I need?

Planning a trek isn't as complicated as you imagine. Trekking has been around for many years and the Nepali people are one of the friendliest and most helpful in the world.

If you're feeling nervous about planning, this book will be your comprehensive guide to trekking in Nepal.

You'll be able to confidently trek through the Nepali mountains after reading this book. It will give you all the tips you need even before landing in Kathmandu, Nepal.

It will cover everything from choosing a mountain to buying gear to completing a trek successfully.

I wrote this book to give you the advice I was given before my trek. My hope is that you'll have a wonderful, challenging, and even life-altering experience in the mountains.

In each chapter, you can find trekking advice on the chapter's topic along with my own personal tips and experience.

Let's begin with choosing a mountain to trek!

Chapter 1: How to Choose Mountain to Trek: Why Manaslu

Before worrying about what gear you need for your trek, you need to choose a time to go and a mountain to trek through.

These first two steps are the most crucial part of your trek preparation. You wouldn't want to go trekking in an unfavorable season or pick a mountain that's too difficult for you.

When to Go Trekking

First, you need to figure out when to go trekking. The timing is everything to you as a trekker. It can determine what extra gear you may need and affect your overall experience.

Strictly speaking, you can go on a trek any time of the year; however, fall and spring are the two peak seasons. It's recommended to go during one of the peak seasons-especially as a new trekker- since there will be more people to help you.

- **Fall (October-November):** Fall season is the most popular trekking season and possibly the best. Fall immediately follows the monsoon season so the weather will be nearly perfect. You'll have more sunny days with mild temperatures for a lucid view of the mountains and other landscapes. The downside of this season is the number of people on the trails. You'll be sharing the trails with crowds of trekkers depending on the route and mountain you choose.

- **Spring (March-April):** Spring season is the second most popular trekking season. During the spring, you can see giant-sized rhododendron trees blooming in the foreground of the mountains as you walk on the trails. This season brings mild temperatures to see Nepali wildlife. Just as the fall trekking season, tourists flock to the trails making them busy and crowded. In the lower altitudes, you may have foggy views which clear up as you trek higher.

- **Off-Season:** Trekking during the off-season has its advantages. You won't need to share the trails with hordes of people and it might make befriending the locals easier. During the off season, trekking prices go down significantly as well. There are disadvantages to trekking in solitude so don't be indifferent when you choose your trekking dates.

- **Winter (December-February):** Winter season is for the more experienced trekkers. You can still have clear days with excellent mountain views as the other trekking seasons. However, be aware that the temperatures during this time are harsh and there's a chance of a winter storm interrupting your plans with little notice. On top of the unpredictable weather conditions, you don't have many daylight hours during the trek. Also, park officials close many of the popular routes and treks for safety. Additionally, some routes are inaccessible due to heavy snowfall.

- **Monsoon (May-September):** The monsoon season is not the best time to go trekking. Remember, the monsoon season brings heavy rainfall which can cause landslides and bring leaches to the surface. The landslides make the trails difficult and even dangerous to be on and the leaches are just annoying. During the monsoon season, the weather is hot and humid and you won't get a clear view of the mountains.

I went on my trek during the fall trekking season and extremely happy that I did. While I was in Kathmandu, there was a constant flow of trekkers coming from or going on a trek. Everyone I met in my hostel was happy to give me advice or answer my questions.

On the trails, I enjoyed seeing and connecting with familiar faces. The other trekkers helped keep me motivated when things became harder for me at high altitudes.

Other Treks

While I will primarily focus on trekking through the Manaslu mountains, I do want to describe other treks that you could choose.

I realize Manaslu might not be the trek for you so I want to offer an overview of other treks you can go on.

Kangchenjunga Trek

The Kanchenjunga mountain range is located in Nepal and India. Its summit reaches 8,586 meters and ranks as the third highest mountain in the world.

On the trails, you can see wildlife ranging from red pandas to snow leopards.

You'll begin the trek in welcoming and intriguing bamboo forests, transition to more rocky landscapes with pine trees, and finally, trek through snow-capped mountains.

Spring is the best time to trek through the Kangchenjunga mountains. You can see a variety of trees and flowers in bloom and if you get lucky a snow leopard.

Upper Mustang Trek

The Upper Mustang trek is located near the Annapurna Circuit trek. It's actually a waterless river valley where you can trek anywhere from 3,000-4,000 meters.

On the trails, you'll trek through a barren desert landscape where you can see mountain peaks and cliffs with caves carved into them.

On this trek, there isn't much variety in terms of landscape. However, it's a unique experience to trek through a barren desert with caves and mountain peaks surrounding you.

Unlike other treks, you'll experience more Tibetan than Nepali culture.

Spring, monsoon, and fall are the best times to trek through the Upper Mustang. Since the route is in the rain shadow of the mountains, it's an ideal monsoon and year-round trek.

Three Passes Trek

The three passes trek takes you through Kogma La, Cho La, and Renjo La in the Everest base camp region. While you won't climb to the summit, the trek will take you up to 5,335 meters altitude.

On the trails, you slowly become closer to the world's highest mountains through the complete Everest area.

Unlike trekking to Everest base camp, you'll have fewer people on the trails, which might be more pleasant for you.

The main attraction of the Three Passes trek is seeing and being surrounded by the mountains for miles.

Spring and fall are the best seasons to trek through the Three Passes. These seasons will guarantee moderate weather for clear and breath-taking views of the mountains.

Dhaulagiri Circuit Trek

The Dhaulagiri Circuit trek is located west of the Annapurna Circuit trek. This trek takes you through the Dhaulagiri Mountains and a few other Himalayan mountains. You'll trek up to 5,000 m altitude.

On the trails, you'll begin trekking through Nepali farmland and then through steep and rocky snow-covered mountains. The higher you trek, the fewer permanent villages you'll see.

This trek is particularly challenging since you'll spend at least three nights sleeping at or above 5,000 meters. The descent in some passes is also very steep with loose rocks and stones.

Dhaulagiri is not for beginner trekkers since it may turn into a technical climb when you cross over the glacier. Additional gear needed includes crampons, ice-axes, and rope for the glacier crossing.

Spring and fall are the best seasons to embark on this trek. You'll have nearly perfect weather and clear skies for the mountain views you want.

Annapurna Dhaulagiri Trek

The Annapurna Dhaulagiri trek is located west of the Annapurna Sanctuary route and close to the Poon Hill region. This trek won't take you nearly as high as other ones, but 3, 650 meters is still no small feat.

On the trails, you'll first see flourishing green forests and split-leveled fields encircling Nepali villages. In the background, you'll have a wide outlook on the mountains.

If you want a structured and well-managed trekking experience then this trek is what you're looking for. Along the trails, you'll find homestays and community-structured projects you can be a part of.

It's one of the best treks for beginner trekkers or those who don't want to be so far removed from their comforts.

Spring and fall are the best seasons for this trek.

Annapurna Circuit Trek

The Annapurna Circuit trek is located in the Annapurna mountains and takes you up to 5,415 meters altitude.

On the trails, you'll see a variety of plants, landscapes, and animals as you make your way up and then back down. You'll start in jungle rainforests and then move towards the snow-capped mountains.

You'll be able to see alluring views of the Annapurna, Macchupurrchre, Dhaulagiri, Manaslu, and Langtang Himal mountains.

It's an ideal trek if you want a route that attracts other trekkers you can easily meet on the trails and tea houses.

Spring and fall are the best seasons for this trek. In the fall season, you'll meet Annapurna Circuit trekkers in Kathmandu even before starting.

Rara Lake Trek

The Rara Lake trek is located in the western Himalayan mountains in the Karnali region and takes you to 3,200 meters altitude.

The trails on this trek won't take you up to the snow-capped mountains. However, it does take you through a forested wilderness, where black bears and musk deer roam. You'll also pass through villages on your way to Rara Lake.

This trek offers a different experience of Nepali culture since it is very much off the beaten path.

If you want to have a trek centered more on solitude and wilderness, this is the one for you. It's rumored that Rara Lake has more birds than the number of trekkers that come through each year.

Spring and fall are the best seasons to go especially if you want to see as many birds as possible.

Annapurna Base Camp Trek

Annapurna Base Camp trek-also known as the Annapurna Sanctuary Trek. This trek takes you through the Annapurna mountains up to 4,130 meters altitude.

Similar to the Annapurna Circuit trek, you can see a variety of plants and animals on the trails. Right from the start of this trek, you'll be able to see snow-capped mountains in the distance, even when you start in the rainforest landscape.

This is one of the most popular treks and ideal if you want the company of other trekkers the entire time.

Spring and fall are the best seasons for the Annapurna Base Camp trek for the same reason as the Annapurna Circuit Trek.

Makalu Base Camp Trek

Makalu Base Camp trek takes you through the Makalu mountains up to 5,5517 meters altitude.

On the trails, you'll see and pass sites similar to Annapurna Dhaulagiri trek. You can expect attractions such as split-level farmlands, glaciers, and waterfalls, and of course snow-capped mountains.

What makes this trek standout is its ruggedness and the opportunity to experience the Rai and Sherpa culture of eastern Nepal.

This trek is not as popular as others since parts of its route can be inaccessible due to the weather conditions. Having said that, it's not the most difficult trek either.

It's not recommended for beginner trekkers due to the ruggedness and primitive conditions.

Spring and fall are the best seasons for Makalu Base Camp trek since the weather will be more suitable for long days on the trails. During these seasons, the trails will be fully accessible to you.

Upper Dolpo Trek

The Upper Dolpo Trek is located in western Nepal in the Dolpo mountains. This trek takes you up to 5,350 meters altitude. Be aware that this trek is considered one the most remote ones, but don't let that stop you from embarking on it.

On the trails and throughout the trek, you'll see Buddhist monasteries, and possibly a snow leopard, and turquoise lakes.

Highlights include Lake Phoksundo and Shey Gompa, and a Buddhist monastery.

Similar to the Makalu trek, the Upper Dolpo trek is quite remote with very few travelers on it. The tourism industry is not quite as developed as other treks so you need to bring camping gear with you and food.

Spring and fall are the best seasons to trek. Although you might not find many people on the trails, the temperate weather conditions will make your camping experience more pleasant.

Langtang Valley Trek

The Langtang Valley is located in the Langtang Valley region not very far from Kathmandu and takes you to 4,700 meters altitude at the most.

This might be one the most underrated trek since it doesn't have as high altitudes as other treks. However, the landscape of this trek is one of its kind and is truly a great opportunity to see it for yourself.

The landscape is beautiful and has a variety of flora and fauna that line the villages and trails, which makes this trek uniquely special.

Spring and fall are the best seasons to go on this trek.

Why Trek Manaslu

Trekking through the Manaslu mountains combines the features of the popular treks such as Everest Basecamp with the remoteness and solitude of the Upper Dolpo trek.

Starting in the 1990s, trekkers were permitted to hike through the Manaslu region, but after the 2015 Earthquake, it was temporarily shut down.

Two years after the earthquake, the trails opened up again and trekkers chose this over Annapurna or Everest for its challenge, scenic views, and less busy trails.

The Manaslu Circuit trek is located east of the Annapurna mountains. You'll trek through alluring rainforests, rocky landscapes, valleys surrounded by mountains, and finally snow-capped mountains.

On this trek, you'll hike around the Manaslu Mountains and ascend up and through Larkya La Pass. At Larkya La Pass, you'll see panoramic views of not only the Manaslu Mountains but also the Himlung Himal, Cheo Himal, Kang Guru, and Annapurna Mountains.

Being in the presence of majestic nature will humble and bond you with everyone who made the long and rewarding journey with you.

The Larkya La Pass isn't the only highlight on this trek.

This trek is also known for

- Mountainside Buddhist monasteries.
- Luscious jungles in the lower altitudes.
- Burly pines in the rougher landscapes in the middle altitudes.
- Snow-capped mountains in the higher altitudes.
- Buri Gandaki, a long and deep river gorge, with many suspension bridges to cross over.

If this doesn't convince you, imagine this:

You're on the second to last day on the trails. It's the toughest day on the trek but also the most rewarding. You'll finally trek through the Larkya La Pass and reach 5,106 meters altitude. You're cold, tired, and you have a headache and feel nauseous from the Altitude Sickness.

You've been trekking for four hours and it's not even noon yet. You have five more hours on the trails before reaching your final destination. Your trekking companion, guide, and other trekkers on the trails encourage and inspire you to keep going despite your health.

You continue to trek slowly with your guide. As others pass you on the trails, they smile and say a few encouraging words to you.

Finally, you reach the final hill before reaching the Larkya La Pass. You take a deep breath and slowly continue to hike up.

Once you get to the top, everyone is smiling at you and giving you a hug or high-five. You also hug and congratulate other trekkers for making it through the toughest part of the trek. You feel proud of yourself for pushing your limits and overcoming the most challenging part of the trek. The trekker comradery is strong and you couldn't be more grateful for it.

You can relax knowing everything will be easier going forward.

After catching your breath, you take a look at your settings. You find yourself surrounded by mountains for miles. It makes you feel humbled and grateful for the unique opportunity and situation you've found yourself in.

Was it worth the Altitude Sickness and trekking through the frigid weather conditions?

Yes.

It's a once in a lifetime opportunity you'll remember for years to come and it will be something to learn from.

The last excerpt, was an "at glance" of my thoughts during my trek through the Manaslu Mountains. I was very tired and dealing with Altitude Sickness as I made my way through the Larkya La Pass. Reaching the top was a "victory" and made me feel proud of myself. Seeing everyone I met throughout the trek smiling and congratulating me made me feel loved and bonded with them. It was truly a gem I will treasure for a long time.

Trek Lengths

When you're choosing which trek to go on, the length is another factor to consider.

Ask yourself:

- How comfortable am I in remote areas?
- How much time do I have on my vacation?
- How long can I go without contacting my friends and family?

Often, the trek length depends on what you can handle and the trek route.

Take the following examples:

- The Manaslu Circuit Trek takes at least seventeen days to complete, two of which are transportation days to and from Kathmandu. Think about if you want to spend seventeen days in remote areas or if you're comfortable trusting others whom you just met. The tea houses don't have many amenities you're accustomed to. Consider if you can remove yourself from your comforts and still have a fulfilling experience.

- The Annapurna treks have a variation to choose from depending on what you want and your comfort level. You can decide if you'd like a long or a short trek. On most of the Annapurna treks, you'll get a taste of Nepali culture without leaving too many of your own comforts.

- The Everest treks have a slight variation in their lengths. If you're more adventurous and an experienced trekker, you might consider the Three Passes trek. If you want to trek on trails with others, Everest Base Camp is a wonderful way to meet people and enjoy a challenging and rewarding experience.

I chose the Manaslu Circuit Trek since it was challenging, not crowded, and still allowed me to meet people on the trails or tea houses.

Trekking Difficulty Grades

One of the last factors to take into account is a trek's difficulty grade. This is important as you wouldn't want to sign up for a trek you cannot complete or one that's too technical.

Bottom line, choose a trek that is suitable to your fitness and experience level.

The difficulty rating depends on your fitness level, experience, backpack weight, and weather conditions.

Porters are also a factor that determines the overall difficulty level. You can hire a porter or share one to carry your heavy gear. In this case, you'll carry a comfortable day bag with your immediate supplies. This makes the trails more accessible and easier for you.

I'll use what I just discussed as factors that define a trek's difficulty grade.

Easy Trek Grades

An easy trek is for anyone with any level of fitness and trekking experience. You can expect to walk on average six to seven hours a day on the trails.

The highest altitude a trek takes you is around 4,000 meters so there's a low chance you'll get Altitude Sickness. If your fitness level is average, you can complete an easy grade trek.

Ghorepani Poon Hill, a short Everest Trek, Kathmandu region treks, and Annapurna are good examples of easy treks to choose from. Annapurna might be the most challenging of the easy treks, but not out of reach.

Moderate Trek Grades

A moderate trek requires you to be comfortable walking six hours a day at most. It would greatly help if you've had some prior hiking experience or love the outdoors.

The highest altitude a trek could take you is between 3,900 and 4,800 meters altitude. Unlike an easy trek, if you're not careful, you could get Altitude Sickness as you trek higher.

On this type of trek, you'll be trekking on well-managed trails, ascending and descending on stone staircases, and, on occasion, trek on steep gravel trails.

Langtang Valley Trek, Helambu Trek, Annapurna Basecamp Trek, Gokyo Lake Trek, and Everest are all moderate treks.

Challenging or Strenuous Trek Grades

A challenging or strenuous trek absolutely demands excellent physical fitness and good health conditions. You'll be walking for six to seven hours on the trails per day through paths that are not always maintained.

On this trek, you can expect to go up to 5,000 meters altitude or a couple hundred meters more. This is another type of trek where you can get Altitude

Sickness if you've never been up so high or are not careful.

These treks will take you on trails through isolated environments in sometimes very harsh weather conditions. You'll go through high altitudes with very low oxygen content and sleep in very basic accommodations.

Prior trekking and camping experience, being physically and mentally fit is needed to complete this type of trek. In addition to having perseverance and a positive attitude.

Annapurna Base Camp Trek, Everest Base Camp Trek, Gokyo Valley Trek, Manaslu Circuit Trek, and Upper Mustang trek fall into the challenging or strenuous trek grade.

Very Challenging or Strenuous Trek Grade

A very challenging or strenuous trek requires a high level of physical fitness and mountaineering knowledge and prior experience. You'll be walking for at least seven hours on the trails per day.

On this trek, you can expect to go between 5,000 and 6,000 meters altitude at the very least. You'll traverse through rough and rustic trails. As you make your way up to the snow-capped mountains, you'll cross through remote areas and some snow-capped passes.

Accommodations will be similar to other treks in lower altitudes, but expect to stay in tents once you reach around 4,000 meters altitude.

This is a technical trek so additional gear such as axes and crampons is needed for snow covered passes. It's highly recommended to take either a rock climbing, glacier walking, or technical climbing class before going on one of these expeditions.

Everest Base Camp with Island Peak and Everest Base Camp with Mera Peak, are examples of a very challenging or strenuous trek that is a technical climb.

I picked Manaslu since it fell in the challenging grade and it wouldn't be as crowded as Everest or Annapurna. I knew my background and training in triathlons and swimming would give me a good foundation and the trails would challenge my physical and mental fitness.

While I was on the trek, it felt like a perfect fit. My physical and mental fitness was pushed to and past its limits in the best ways possible. I enjoyed the having a little bit of solitude and warmly welcomed a cheerful chat with other trekkers in the tea houses.

Chapter 2: Independent or Guided Trekking

After deciding which mountain to trek, you need to choose whether to trek independently or with a guide. When you get to the root of the choice, it will heavily depend on your personal preference and experience level.

If you've decided to trek independently, read on about the preparation, pros and cons, and a few other tips.

If you're not sure about your experience or preparedness level, then you can skip to the section about guided trekking and how to find a trekking agency.

Independent Trekking

If you have prior trekking or backpacking experience, you'll be fine trekking without a guide. Especially if you trek through the Everest Basecamp or Annapurna Circuit region. You'll find other trekkers on the trails or even before you leave.

Independent trekking does give you more freedom; however, a guide does more than help you figure out the logistics. A great guide can teach you about the Nepali culture and may even become your friend.

Popular treks such as Everest and Annapurna doesn't require a guide in the regions and parks you trek through. The trails, on these treks, are well marked and maintained leaving little room for error.

Preparing for an Independent Trek

Preparing yourself to trek independently does take more work on your end, but it's manageable if you know what you're doing.

Unlike trekking with a guide, you have to arrange all the transportation, obtain the needed permits and park passes yourself.

You can take care of all these tasks in Kathmandu's Thamel district. This place is full of trekking agencies, travel agencies, and hostels. All which can point you in the right direction.

As an independent trekker, there are a couple things to keep in mind:

- *Money*
  Make sure you take the right amount of cash and keep it in a couple safe spots. Once you leave Kathmandu, you won't see an ATM until you return. You'll be responsible for your own food and proper lodging if you're staying in tea houses.

- *Backpack*
  Unless you hire a porter, you'll carry all of your gear for hours each day on rocky trails. Buy or rent a comfortable backpack that can carry

your heavy and light gear. To make things more pleasant, only bring the bare minimum. After a couple days, you won't want to carry all the gear anyway.

Independent Trekking Pros

- *Choose your own itinerary*
  You're the boss of your trek. You can decide when to leave and come back. Let's say that you thought you needed two days to prepare for Everest Basecamp. In reality, you actually needed three. As an independent trekker, you have the flexibility to give yourself that third day.
  On the trek, you can set your own pace and spend more time in one village if you want. If you need an extra day to acclimatize to the altitude, you can continue when you're ready.

- *Cheaper Option*
  Trekking independently is cheaper than going through an agency or hiring a guide. You can save money and buy more food and other "treats" such as hot water or a nice meal.

- *Pick Where to Sleep*
  As an independent trekker, you can choose where to sleep every night. If there's a specific lodge that has great reviews you can go there.

- *Meet More Trekkers*

Independent trekking forces you to talk to locals and other trekkers on the trails. You'll pick up a few new tips and perhaps a new friend.

- *Learn to Speak the Native Language*
  You don't need to be fluent in Nepali to trek independently. However, knowing a few words goes a long way when you first arrive at a tea house.

Independent Trekking Cons

- *Health and Safety Concerns*
  This is one of the biggest cons when it comes to independent trekking.
  If you become severely ill or injured, you might need a helicopter evacuation. Helicopters won't come unless there is a guaranteed cash payment. Usually, a trekking agency arranges this and it's included with their fee.
  As an independent trekker, you need to show proof of a cash payment through a credit card or your embassy. Tea houses and local law enforcement are able to help you get in touch with an embassy if needed.
  On the trails, you need to be careful if you're alone. If you become injured, you'll have to wait for the next person to come along to get help. Keep in mind, you won't have a signal for your phone.

- *Finding a Place to Sleep*

During the high trekking seasons, you might have trouble getting a room if you're alone or in a small group. Trekking agencies get preference at tea houses.

There is a way around this situation though. On the popular routes, there are tea houses that usually host large groups. Try to plan around those houses. There are tea houses an hour walk away from the popular ones. Buy a guidebook with an extensive list of tea houses and popularity ratings.

Worst case scenario, you sleep in the dining hall. It's not as bad as it sounds since it is usually warmer than the sleeping rooms. Tea houses, don't turn away people so the dining hall may be the only space that's left.

- *More Time Spent on Logistics*
  As an independent trekker, you are completely accountable for gear, permits, and arranging transportation. If you want to hire a guide or porter outside of an agency, then you're responsible for them as well as yourself. Organizing a trek on a popular route won't be as extensive or time-consuming as a remote one, but do be prepared for it.

- *Limited Information*
  You have limited information if you're an independent trekker. You're in a new place and you might not know all the customs, etiquettes, and routes. A guide would tell you this information and you'd just have to follow his directions.

If you go with an open mind and do research beforehand, you should be fine on the trek. If you aren't sure about anything, ask someone in the tea house or even on the trails.

Guided Trekking

Going on a guided trek is the best option if you've never been on a trek or are nervous about being in remote areas.

Remember, a guide does more than just help you with the trek logistics, park and trail information, and safety on the trek. They can teach you about the Nepali culture and may even become your friend.

Preparing for a guided trek doesn't take nearly as much work on your part as an independent trek. Most of the work is finding a reputable trekking agency and guide which can easily be done in Kathmandu, or even before you get there.

After finding a reputable trekking agency, all you have to worry about is finding the right gear for your trek.

I'll discuss how to find a reputable trekking agency and guide in the coming sections.

For now, I'll go on about the pros and cons of doing a guided trek.

Guided Trekking Pros

- *Pre-Trip Details*
  When you trek with a guide through a trekking agency all the trek's details are taken care of. You won't have to obtain any park or trekking fees yourself. The trekking agency will do it for you. The most you'll need to provide is a copy of your passport photo to make trekking permits.

- *Transportation*
  Although you'll land in Kathmandu, Nepal, your trek won't start from there. You'll have to ride a jeep, bus, or even take a plane to the start location. Independent trekkers need to take care of these details themselves. A trekking agency has deals with local and even private bus companies and will arrange your transportation to and from Kathmandu.

- *Hiking Details*
  On the trails, you won't have to worry about where you're going, lodging for the night, and even food. Your guide is very knowledgeable about which lodges to go to and what the route looks like. Keep in mind, the guide has been on the trek many times and has lead different skill-leveled trekkers.
  Your guide will also keep you on an evenly-paced schedule so you can trek safely.

- *Safety Tips*
  Adhering to safety tips is especially important when you get to higher altitudes. Some people

may do just fine while others will have some difficulty. Listening to your guide will help you safely trek through higher altitudes.
Your guide will also know how to navigate unsafe passages on the trails.

- *Cultural Insights*
Since your guide is from Nepal, he can give you insights on his culture and everyday life in the mountain villages. If you want to know more about the Buddhist religion and the monks who journey to the monasteries, he will be able to provide some direction in that area.

- *Emergency Situations*
A guide also can be your trekking companion. If you become injured or sick he can help you get better. If you need to be airlifted, all the costs will have already been paid through the trekking agency.

Guided Trekking Cons

- *More Expensive*
Guided treks cost money for its service, information, guide, and porter if you hire one. Consider what your money is going towards. It covers nearly all your meals and lodging, which helps the local economy and the tourism business.

- *No Flexibility in the Schedule*

To keep the group on schedule and to be as efficient as possible, a guide must follow a schedule with little room for flexibility.
If you need an extra day to acclimatize to the altitude you might need to push through until you get to lower altitudes. It's unfortunate but you paid for a set number of days with your guide.
You also don't have the freedom to take extra days to explore an area you find interesting or go on an excursion.

- *Trekking with Strangers*
Sometimes, you find yourself in a group with strangers, which can be uncomfortable at first. However, think of it this way: you're going to meet other trekkers on the trails anyway so why not start with the people in your group? You'll bond with them after being in the mountains for a couple weeks along with other trekkers you meet.

- *The Group Stays Together*
The guide is responsible for his trekkers. It would be rare if he allows you to wander by yourself or start earlier than the group.
This also means that if there's someone slower in the group, the guide cannot leave him or her behind. You have to go at their pace and encourage them to keep going.

Selecting a Trekking Agency

If you've decided to go on a guided trek, the next part is selecting a trekking agency.

Similar to other topics I've discussed this is also important. It can affect your overall experience on the trek.

It's not a trekking agency's office staff you have to worry about. It's their guides and porters they put on the trails with you.

It's hard to choose a trekking agency since there's so many. If you land in Kathmandu without a clue, every businessman will claim his agency is the best or the most reputable.

I spent a lot of time researching different trekking agencies online before landing in Kathmandu. It was worth the effort since I knew exactly where to book my guide and porter.

I narrowed down my search using five factors to help compare trekking agencies to each other.

Five Factors to Look for in Every Trekking Agency

1. *Number of Years in Business and Knowledge*
   The older agencies tend to be better than the younger ones. An older agency tends to be more knowledgeable and reliable. Look for

agencies that are least ten to fifteen years old.

2. *Client Testimonials and Reviews*
   Read all the previous client's testimonials and reviews. A business, no matter the industry, cannot sustain itself without positive reviews. TripAdvisor and Lonely Planet are good places to begin your review search.

3. *Association*
   If an agency is affiliated with Government or Non-Government organizations, it classifies its reliability level. Its affiliation is also telling of its Corporate Social Responsibility (CSR) tactics.

4. *Registration and Licenses*
   A trekking agency cannot legally run their business without the proper registration and licenses. An agency needs a registration from the Nepal government, Nepal Tourism Board (NTB), and Trekking Agencies' Association of Nepal (TAAN). If a trekking agency sells or rents climbing gear then it also needs to register with the Nepal Mountaineering Association (NMA).

5. *Pricing and Facilities*
   You can't depend on price to be the primary indicator of an agency's quality. You'll determine what a "reasonable" price is from doing company comparisons. Facilities also become a big decision of whether to sign on with the trekking agency. Facilities include pick-up and drop services, accommodation before or after the trek, reliable and

knowledgeable guides, and emergency services if needed.

I used those five factors to help me pick out reliable and long-standing agencies over the ones that were only in business for less than ten years.

After using those five factors, I went through eight steps to pick between my top five agencies.

I repeated a few of these steps from above to emphasize their importance.

Eight Steps to Choose the Best Trekking Agency

1. *Evaluate What You Want and Anticipate*
   When you narrow down your list, begin to write a set of parameters. This can include your budget, comfort level, fitness level, languages spoken, and number of days you want to trek. When you define your needs and constraints it will help you make an informed decision.

2. *Registration, Licenses, and Affiliation*
   This cannot be emphasized enough. A reputable and reliable trekking agency must have the correct registration and licenses to legally run. If you're unsure if a company has the correct registrations, visit TAAN's website which has a list of trekking agencies registered with it.

3. *Client Testimonials and Reviews*
   If you've selected a trekking agency in your top five, then you've determined it has enough positive reviews. When you're reading the reviews a second time, try to get a sense of what the trekking experience is like.

4. *Pricing and Facilities*
   A reasonable price is relative and varies from person to person. To find your reasonable price, compare agencies based on your needs and constraints for the trek with the facilities offered. Remember, facilities include responsible and reputable guides and emergency rescue in the worst-case scenario.

5. *Email the Agency*
   Send an email inquiry to multiple trekking agencies and ask very specific questions about their services and facilities. Communicating with them will not only clarify any questions you have, you'll also know the company more closely.

6. *Safety Standards*
   Trekking is generally a strenuous and challenging activity not a dangerous one. If you're not careful it can become risky. To ensure your own safety, check the trekking agency's safety standards and records. Ask what emergency services they provide.

7. *Trekking Agencies and their Guides*
   Your guide will make the biggest difference on your trek. Remember, you might be traveling through the mountains for three weeks. It's

absolutely imperative that the trekking agency has guides with valid guide certificates, insurance, and gear. This ensures that your guide has been trained and that safety is also prioritized for your guide too. If you don't speak English, you may need to search for a multi-lingual trekking agency.

8. *Interview the Guides*
   If you get the chance to "interview" various guides, just do it. You'll be glad you did and it can make a difference once you start trekking on the trails. It can help you narrow down and choose which one of them will match your personality and if you two can communicate well. During the high season, guides are put on the next trek that's available to them so you might not have many choices. I didn't "interview" the guide who took me through Manaslu, but I got along well with my guide and had a very pleasant time on my trek.

After following these steps, I was able to find an adequate trekking agency and was content with the service and facilities they provided.

Porters and Guides

Seeing porters and guides on your trek is fairly common and the rates for them can be quite competitive.

Generally speaking, you can expect to pay $25-30 per day for a guide and $10-15 per day for a porter.

A guide's role, as mentioned earlier, is to help with the trek's logistics, trail information, Nepali nature and culture, and safety.

If you decide to trek with a guide, be sure that they can speak English since they'll be your main person of contact on the trek. They'll organize transportation to and from Kathmandu, lodging, food and drinks, hiking schedule, and trail route.

If you have any questions regarding Nepali culture, customs, festivals, and everyday life, your guide would be the person to ask. You and your guide may even become lifelong friends by the end of the trek.

A porter's role is to carry your heavy gear so you can carry a small day bag with your immediate essentials.

Porters are just as useful and important on the trails as the guides. They sometimes serve as back up guides or are training to become one themselves. Porters are especially helpful to older and beginner trekkers.

If you do hire a porter, keep your heavy gear weight to a minimum. Porters walk the same path as you, so please don't make their job any harder than it is. Keep your bag between 20-30 kg.

How to Choose a Guide

As I mentioned in the previous section, if you get a chance to interview a guide, take advantage of it. Try to interview at least three guides, whether you're hiring through an agency or hiring independently.

Keep in mind, you'll be with this person for possibly three weeks!

When you do an interview with your guide, here are suggested questions to ask and verify.

- Verify and agree on the route.
- Settle on a price.
- Agree on who will be responsible for a porter, if you hire one. This question is mainly for insurance purposes. You'll only have to worry about this if you've decided to trek independently.
- Inquire how many times the guide has been on the trek.
- If you're comfortable, ask what else they do aside from being a guide. This is a way for you to get to know their personality.
- Verify who pays for what on the trek. This is another factor, you'll only have to worry about if you've decided to trek independently.
- Verify that they have the correct registration and licenses and that they are insured.
- Inquire if your guide will want to drink on the trek at the tea houses. Only ask if this would be an issue for you.
- Verify that your guide will be financing his own food and lodging expenses.

- Always double check finances before leaving the interview.
- At the end of the interview, ask yourself if you are content and comfortable with the guide.

Remember, it doesn't all have to be business questions, try to figure out if your personalities will work together.

As I mentioned earlier, I didn't interview my guide, but I still enjoyed my trek a lot and felt fulfilled.

What to Know When Trekking with a Guide

A handful of your guide's duties depends on what you agreed on before hiring him.

These are just a few things that your guide may do while you're on the trek:

- Your guide can help you obtain any permits or park passes before the trek.

- Your guide gets a percentage of the profits from the tea houses so they will pay a significantly lower rate than you.

- The cost of food and water goes up the higher you trek since it takes more time and effort to transport those things there.

- Tipping is not a part of the Nepali culture; however, until 20 years ago no one tipped the guides and porters. Now, it is almost expected to tip your guide and porter. Generally, you tip your guide 10% of the price agreed on and 5% if you hired a porter. Be sure your guide shares the tip with the porter. Tipping is not mandatory and it's completely based on how well you felt your guide took you through the trek.

- You're 100% responsible for preparing for your trek. That means buying the right gear for lower and higher altitudes, bringing enough cash, and being physically fit before leaving. Your guide can offer his own advice and help, but ultimately, it's you who creates your unique trekking experience.

How to Find Trekking Companions

Some people are wired to do adventurous things solo while others want a companion. There's nothing wrong with either scenario as it is preference based.

In this section, I'll quickly review the advantages of traveling with a companion (not including your guide) and the situations where a trekking companion is most needed.

Keep in mind, that solo trekking is legal but not for everyone.

Here is a quick reminder of why having a trekking companion is good:

- It's safer to have someone with you on the trails. If you become sick, it can relieve some of the pressure from the guide. A trekking companion promotes comradery and community on the trails, which is important when you trek in higher altitudes.

- It's more fun with a trekking companion. After the trek is complete, you can share the adventure between you and your trekking companion(s).

- It's less expensive to trek with a companion. You and a companion or two can split the cost of a guide or share a porter and bring less clothing.

- "Restricted Trekking Permits" require that you trek with someone else. The Upper Mustang, Upper Dolpo, Manaslu, and Makalu Basecamp are examples of treks that have this permit.

Finding Your Trekking Companion

Finding a trekking companion is not as hard as you think. You can easily find one in your hostel in or even on the plane ride over!

If you're really nervous about it, you can sign up to do a trek with a trekking agency. Nearly all trekking agencies organize group tours and will gladly add you if there's room.

Just as finding a guide, you can do an informal "interview" with a potential trekking companion. You want to be sure that you'll be compatible and communicate well with each other.

If you're unsure about what else to look for in a trekking companion, here is a list of suggested attributes to look for.

- *Complementary Skills*
  Ideally, you and a trekking companion have complementary skills and can potentially learn from each other.

- *Shares Expectations*
  A "fulfilling" trek means something different to everyone. If you want to take more excursions on the trek and try to understand the Nepali culture, then look for someone who shares those values.

- *Open Communication*
  Talking comfortably with your trekking companion is important. It can help you through surprising challenges and even help motivate each other at higher altitudes.

- *Fitness Level*
  A trekking companion implies that it's someone who treks alongside you most of the

way. Trekking with someone who is far slower than you could put a strain on your patience. On the other side, someone who is blazing the trails could leave you exhausted at the end of your days. This also may cause you to develop injuries from over-exertion.

- *Trustworthy*
  Finding someone who is trustworthy is the most important attribute in a trekking companion. Imagine if you become injured or the weather turns sour. Can you trust this person to make sound decisions and listen to your thoughts?

- *Enjoy Spending Time Together*
  You'll be spending almost three weeks with your trekking companion so make sure you like being around them. Ask yourself if you can chat with them easily or be in silence when you need it.

Of course, no one will have all of these attributes to make an ideal trekking companion. However, I hope these will help you pick someone to go on a once-in-a-lifetime adventure.

I fell into the category of being nervous about finding a trekking companion. I decided to join an existing the Manaslu Circuit trek group. I met my trekking companion the day we left and by the end, we were good friends! Since my trekking companion and I weren't friends before the trek, it pushed me to talk to her and other trekkers.

Chapter 3: How to Prepare for Manaslu

Believe or not, you can wait until you arrive in Nepal to prepare! You won't want to carry all the trekking gear on your journey to Nepal. It's too much of a hassle and can be expensive.

It's cheaper to buy everything you need in Kathmandu. After the trek, either ship it home or give it to someone else. One of my hostel roommates gave me his hiking sticks. I ended up using them once and gave it to the next person who needed it.

If you're organizing your trek through a trekking agency, check what gear you can borrow or rent from them. Some gear your guide will have such as a first aid kit so there's no need to buy it.

If you find trekking companions before you leave, you can split costs on a few items such as altitude medication, band-aids, and tiger balm.

I was able to borrow a sleeping bag and down jacket from the trekking agency I used. Otherwise, I had the option to either buy or rent a sleeping bag from one of the many shops in Kathmandu. I bought what I needed and then sent it home when I returned from my trek.

What Gear to Buy

Whether you're trekking independently, in a group, or even with a porter there are key items you need to buy for your trek.

I'll list all the items that were suggested from my trekking agency. I only brought the bare minimum on the trek with me.

You'll get tired of carrying a big backpack full of extraneous items by the middle of the first day on the trails. Remember, it's not easy to send an item back home once you're in the remote mountains!

Suggested Gear List for Tea House Trekking

In this section, I'll list the suggested gear needed for a tea house trek. Remember, on a tea house trek, you'll sleep and eat your meals there. It's also a great place to meet other trekkers.

If you've decided to trek in remote areas, all of the things I'll list and discuss below apply to you. The extra things you need are a tent, sleeping bag, sleeping pad (if you'd like), stove, camp cookware, and any extra camping equipment you want.

Use this list as a checklist as you prepare for your trek and wander around the streets of Kathmandu!

- *Backpack*
  If you're not hiring a porter, don't bring anything heavier than 45L for a tea house trek. Go with something simple and lightweight. Remember, you'll be carrying it around for six hours a day.

- *Sleeping Bag*
  If you're not trekking with an agency, then you will have to rent or buy a sleeping bag. Look for a thermal sleeping bag that can withstand temperatures down to   -20 Centigrade.

  + silk liner !

- *Foot Ware*
  Buying the right shoes for your feet can be tricky. You want something that is sturdy but also light-weight so your legs and feet won't get tired. I decided to use trail running shoes instead of boots. They're more like a running shoe but specifically designed to handle different terrains and are waterproof. If you are more comfortable with boots, go ahead and buy them! Just be sure they are lightweight and you have enough time to break them in.

- *Water Purifier*
  You cannot drink the tap water in Nepal. You need a way to purify your water. You can either buy water purification tablets in Kathmandu or a UV Water Purifier. Both work just the same and you'll be able to drink the water after use.

- *Water Bottles*
  Bring at least two 1L water bottles with you on the trails every day. You can buy good ones in

Kathmandu before leaving. Remember, water fountains aren't abundant on the trails just whenever you stop for food and lodging.

- *Clothing*
Don't over pack and bring the bare minimum. You can sink wash and air out clothes at the tea houses. Try to avoid bringing two items that serve the same purpose and pack in layers. Here is a clothing list I was given from my trekking agency.
  - ✓ *Wind or rain jacket*
  - ✓ *Warm fleece jacket*
  - *Waterproof shell jacket*
  - ✓ *Lightweight gloves*
  - ✓ *Heavyweight gloves or mittens*
  - ✓ *Sun hat or scarf*
  - *Hiking shorts*
  - *T-shirts or tank tops*
  - ✓ *Lightweight cotton long pants*
  - ✓ *Light and expedition weight thermal bottoms*
  - *Fleece or wool pants*
  - ✓ *Rain pants*
  - ✓ *Hiking Socks*
  - *Wool Socks*
  - ✓ *Camp Shoes (sneakers/sandals)* Tent slippers

- *Map, Compass, and Guidebook*
You really need these items if you're trekking without a guide. If you want your own copy of the trek map, you can buy them in Kathmandu or your trekking agency may provide it for you.

[handwritten annotations at top: "nebuli~ / paracetamol", "anti-emetic", "ABX", "plasters", "suture / needle ???", "anti-diarrhoeal."]

- *First-Aid Kit*
  If you're trekking with a guide, he will have a first-aid kit with him, but it's a good idea to bring a small, personalized one to keep in your day bag.

- *Sun Protection*
  If you are sensitive to sunlight, buy sunscreen or a pair of sunglasses. When you are at higher altitudes, the light might bounce off the snow and into your eyes.

- *Head Torches*
  Head torches are useful if you need to make a late night or early morning run to the bathrooms. Most of the time the bathrooms are down the hall and without a light. This item is optional.

- *Pack Cover or Plastic Bags*
  Instead of buying a pack cover, just buy plastic bags to cover your bags when it rains on the trek. You'll also need a plastic bag to keep some of your valuables in your bag dry.

- *Trekking Poles*
  If you have bad or weak knees/ankles, you might want to consider borrowing or buying trekking poles. They can help reduce strain when you have really steep ascents or descents.

- Small Towel
  The tea houses do not have towels so you will have to bring your own. There will be places to

hang dry it.

- *Wristwatch* *(buy a cheap one & leave mine @ home!)*
  Another optional item to bring with you, is a
  watch to keep track of time and elevation
  change. If you're trekking independently, then
  it's a must. The Nepali estimate trekking
  distances in time, not kilometers.

- *Toiletries* *(nails, razor, teeth brush (manual), tooth paste, shaver bar, shampoo, soap)*
  Remember to bring things such as travel-sized
  toothbrush, toothpaste, and personal
  medications. You can buy them if you run out
  or forget but it's more expensive the higher you
  trek.

- *Hand Sanitizer* *— take hand sanitiser*
  You won't always have a sink to wash your
  hands in so bring hand sanitizer for the road. A
  lot of people get sick on Nepal treks so wash
  your hands often and especially before meals.

- *Wet Wipes* *D/W Ben!*
  When you get to the higher altitudes, it
  becomes too cold to shower. Keep in mind the
  shower and bathroom are not well insulated.
  Instead, clean up as best you can with wet
  wipes at the end of the day.

- *Insect Repellent* *D/W Ben!*
  If you're sensitive to bugs, then bring insect
  repellent with you for the lower altitudes. Bring
  repellent with 30% DEET and that should keep
  the bugs off you!

(handwritten: buy @ teahouses!)

- *Toilet Paper*
  Most bathrooms do not have toilet paper so bring enough rolls for the trek. To save room in your bag, take the cardboard out of the roll and squish it down! If you do run out, you can buy more at the tea houses.

- *Gear Repair Tape*

- *Cell phone or Camera*
  You can bring your cell phone on your trek to take pictures. Wifi is becoming more available on the popular treks. I would try to stay off it as much as possible and just use it to take pictures.

(handwritten: ? or pay at teahouses / pw Ben)

- *Power Bank*
  You can bring a power bank if you need to charge your phone. I used my phone maybe three times a day so I never needed to charge mine! My trekking companion had one so I charged it before taking the bus ride back to Kathmandu. If you don't bring it, you can still charge your phone at the tea houses, but you will have to pay a fee for it.

- *Games, Books, and a Journal*
  You'll have more downtime than you think on the trek. You get to the tea houses around 3-4pm and have time before and after dinner to rest, shower, and meet other trekkers. Bring a journal to write down what you did that day or a book to read for alone time. Sharing a game such as cards is a great way to spend time with

someone.

- *Snacks*
  Bring healthy snacks with you and buy them in Kathmandu while the prices are still lower. I went with light snacks such as muesli and peanut butter which I put on my breakfast toast or chapatti!

Ask someone who's been on a trek, "If I don't bring X, will I still be able to enjoy my trek?" This question will help narrow down your list easily. A lot of the items are nice to have but you could do without them. What I thought was unnecessary on my trek could be higher on your priority list.

I didn't take that much and was glad I did! I didn't have to keep track of many things and it made it easier for my porter. *\ she had a porter !*

Where to Buy the Gear

After you've talked to your trekking agency, experienced trekkers, and narrowed down your list, you can go shopping for what you need.

You have a few options for where to buy your gear. Either in your home country, in another country before traveling to Nepal, or in Nepal. The last option is the best and the most cost-effective one!

The only item I'd buy prior to arriving in Kathmandu is your foot ware. The last thing you want is for your boots to give you blisters or make your feet ache on the first day of a seventeen-day trek.

Shopping in Kathmandu

Reserve a bed in a hostel or hotel in the Kathmandu's Thamel district, where all the trekkers first go. The place is full of shops selling every type of trekking, camping, and outdoor gear you could think of and more.

Many of the items you see in the shops is a knock-off from a brand name. The problem you have as a trekker is not the number of items available but the quality of them. The shops sell very inexpensive knock-off gear made from the lowest quality.

It's not a problem if you want to buy non-critical items for your trek. Buying knock-off brands for items such as t-shirts, sandals, and a sun hat are ok and won't affect your experience.

You really want to look carefully and be wary of really cheap deals when you're buying trekking or camping gear. All of which you depend on to keep you warm at higher altitudes or safe during the trek.

In the following two sections, I'll summarize how to find and rent reliable trekking gear and purchase from the brand names.

Renting Reliable Trekking Gear

Renting gear is the best option if you're trekking on a budget. Especially, if you're intending to use the gear once.

Look for the small warehouse-type shops in Kathmandu's Thamel district. These types of shops let trekkers rent reliable and real trekking equipment. Warehouse-type shops recycle authentic gear specifically designed to withstand the cold temperatures in the Nepali mountains.

For example, you may want to rent your down jacket or thermal sleeping bag for the higher altitudes. You can do this for as low as a dollar per day and then return at the end of your trek.

If you don't know where to find a good warehouse-type shop, ask your trekking agency or someone you meet in the hostel. Most trekking agencies have deals with authentic rental shops or will help you find one.

Once you find an authentic rental shop, it won't be hard to separate high and low-quality made gear. To make sure the gear is good, check the logo to start and check if the thermal items still have a good fill. Older items tend to wear out from use over the years. Don't hesitate to ask about other options available.

Purchasing from Brand Names

Since there is such a high demand for trekking gear, the brand name outdoor and adventure gear companies have opened a store in Kathmandu.

Talk a walk down Tridevi Sadak, a short distance from central Thamel, where you can find anything that you missed in Thamel. Only here, it's promised to be the real thing.

To save yourself time, here are the best places to look for trekking gear located on Tridevi Sadak

- *Red Fox*
  Red Fox is a Russian company that caters more to mountaineering than trekking gear. If you're looking for extreme cold weather gear this is the place to buy it. It also specializes in tents and sleeping bags for high altitudes.

- *Sherpa*
  Sherpa is a Sherpa-owned business that makes nearly all of its products in Nepal. It wants to keep things local and contribute to the economy. The brand sells everything from mountain climbing gear to hand-knit scarves.

- *North Face*
  North Face is an American brand that offers outdoor gear for almost any adventure. You can find almost the same products that are offered in other countries. North Face's store in Nepal is tailored more towards outdoor

clothing than trekking gear.

- *Black Yak*
  Black Yak is a South Korean brand that offers adventure gear. It offers quality gear with a distinguishing Himalayan yak logo and vibrant colors.

This list isn't extensive, but it does cover a few of the best and frequently bought brands. Other brands to check out on Tridevi Sadak include Mountain Hardwear, Sonoman, Everest Hard Wear, Mammut, and Salewa.

If you're still unsure of where to shop, ask trekkers you meet in your hostel, your trekking agency, or even the hostel staff. Remember, Nepali people have been trekking for years and their knowledge is quite extensive.

Visa Lengths and Fees

Nepal's government requires that everyone apply for and obtain a tourist visa.

You can apply for the visa prior to landing in Kathmandu by mailing an application and additional documents to the Nepali Embassy. You also have the option to obtain a tourist visa upon arrival.

It's absolutely critical that you get a visa that allows enough time for your trek and any additional days you want to have in the country.

In this section, I'll cover how to obtain a tourist visa for both methods.

Obtaining a Visa through a Consulate

To obtain a visa through a consulate, you need to complete and mail in a visa application form. This can easily be found on Nepal's Embassy website.

You'll also have to send in additional documents which depend on if you're traveling with a passport or travel documents.

If you're a passport holder, you'll need to send in these documents to the Nepali Embassy or consulate:

- Actual Passport with at least six months validity.
- Passport with at least two blank visa pages.
- One copy of the passport identification page.
- One recent passport-sized photograph.
- Completed and signed visa application form.
- Prepaid return envelope with tracking number.

If you're a travel document holder, you'll need to send in these documents to the Nepali Embassy or consulate:

- Actual travel document with at least six months availability.
- At least two blank visa pages left.
- One copy of the travel document identification page.

- One recent passport-sized photograph.
- Completed and signed visa application form.
- Self-signed sponsorship letter by a Nepali citizen.
- Copy of the citizen certificate belonging to the sponsor.
- Prepaid return envelope with tracking number.

Obtaining a Visa Upon Arrival

If you're planning to obtain a visa upon arrival, you'll either apply for it at the Tribhuvan International Airport, in Kathmandu, or at one of overland border points of entry:

- Kakarvitta, Jhapa District.
- Birgunj, Parsa District.
- Kodari, Sindhupalchowk District.
- Balahia, Bhairahawa (Rupandehi District).
- Jamunaha, Nepalgunj (Banke District).
- Mohana, Dhangadhi (Kailali District).
- Gadda Chauki, Mahendran (Kanchanpur District).

The Department of Immigration allows only the Tribhuvan International Airport to issue a visa upon arrival via air travel.

The "on arrival" visa system is very easy to follow and doesn't take too much time. However, during the peak trekking seasons, there might be a line to get your visa.

The visa upon arrival is the same thing as a tourist visa and allows for multiple entries if you need it. If your purpose is solely trekking, you still apply for the tourist visa to get into the country.

Visa Upon Arrival Overland

To get a visa upon arrival by crossing the borders is straightforward as any border crossing. The procedure is the same no matter which border of Nepal you use.

Once you arrive at the border, you'll get off your mode of transportation and collect your bags. After, you'll see a fleet of rickshaws standing outside the bus or train station. They all know you need to go to the immigration office and will take you there.

Once in the immigration office, hand over the needed documents and visa fees to the immigration officer who will process your visa.

After you get your visa, buy the next bus or train ticket to Kathmandu. Or if you like, get to Kathmandu by hitchhiking.

Visa Upon Arrival at the Airport

Once you arrive at the airport follow these steps to get your tourist visa upon arrival.

- Step One

- o Complete the Arrival Card
- o Complete the tourist visa form. If you'd like to speed up this step, you can fill out the tourist visa form before landing. You can find it on Nepal's Department of Immigration website easily. After completing the form online, you'll receive a receipt with a barcode. This document you must print out and have at hand when you go obtain your tourist visa upon arrival. This receipt is valid for 15 days.
- Step Two
  - o Make the cash payment according to your visa length requirement. A visa can be had for fifteen, thirty, and ninety days.
  - o Obtain your receipt.
  - o **Just to note: There aren't any ATMs in immigration and credit cards can be unreliable. Bring the right amount of cash with you and then exchange after immigration.**
  - o Visa upon arrival fees:
    15 days- 25 USD
    30 days- 40 USD
    90 days- 100 USD
- Step Three
  - o Walk to the immigration desk with all your paperwork, payment receipts, and passport.
  - o Give the immigration officer your documents so they can process the visa.

Park and Permit Fees

Anyone who goes on a trek in Nepal needs to obtain and pay for park and trekking permits. The specific type of permit you need depends on the region you're trekking through. You can obtain the permits in Kathmandu or Pokhara before the trek and others on the spot.

For purposes of this book, I'll first give a quick overview of all the types of trekking permits and park fees. Next, I'll specify which ones are needed for Manaslu and how to obtain them.

Trekking Permits

There are four types of permits trekkers will have to obtain before or at the time needed during the trek. Remember, not every trekker will need all four.

- *Special/Restricted Access Trekking Permit* Special trekking permits are needed for trekkers going to restricted or controlled areas. If you aren't trekking through Everest, Annapurna, Langtang, or Helambu, then you'll need to obtain this permit.

  Nepal's Department of Immigration issue these special trekking permits and need to be obtained before embarking on the trek.

  In restricted access areas, trekkers are prohibited from going without a guide and the permits are only issued for groups of two or more persons.

This type of permit can only be gotten through a trekking or travel agency that is recognized by the Department of Immigration.

- *Trekkers Information Management System (TIMS) Card*
A TIMS card is needed in areas where a trekking permit is not needed. These cards help the Nepali government keep track of the trekkers. Doing so helps increase safety and security.

  If a natural disaster happens (snow storm or landslide) or an accident occurs, the information on your TIMS card will help a search and rescue team find trekkers.
For this permit, there are two types of cards, a green card for independent trekkers and a blue card for trekkers with a trekking agency.

  This permit has to be obtained before the trek. If you're trekking with an agency, you'll give them two passport-sized photos and they will take care of the rest of the procedure.

  For independent trekkers, you'll need to complete a TIMS application form and provide two passport-sized photos at the offices of Nepal Tourism Board in Kathmandu.

- *Conservation Area Entrance Permit Fee*
Many treks enter one of Nepal's many national

parks that require a fee for entrance.

Here is a brief list of Nepal's National Parks

- o Sagarmatha National Park
- o Langtang National Park
- o Makalu Barun National Park
- o Rara National Park
- o Shey-Phoksundo National Park
- o Chitwan National Park
- o Khaptad National Park
- o Bardiya National Park
- o Shivapuri National Park

In addition to the national parks, some treks might take you through wildlife reserves such as

- o Shukla Panta Wildlife Reserve
- o Koshi Tappu Wildlife Reserve
- o Parsi Wildlife Reserve

If you're trekking with an agency, they'll already know which national park and wildlife reserve entrance fees you'll need. If you're an independent trekker, check what route you'll go on, and bring enough cash with you for the entrance fees.

- *Peak Climbing and Mountaineering Permit*
  If you're planning to do a technical climb that involves climbing peaks and mountaineering, it needs to be arranged through a trekking agency. The Nepali government has prohibited anyone from peak climbing individually, for safety reasons.

For this permit, you'll need to complete a bio-data form and give it to your trekking agency. You can complete this form online and then sign and attach your photograph to the form when you come to Kathmandu.

Permits and Park Entrance Fees for the Manaslu Trek

For the Manaslu Trek, you'll need two of the four permits and park entrance fees I discussed in the previous section.

Here are the two permits and park entrance fees you'll need:

- Special/Restricted Access Trekking Permit for the Manaslu region. *via Trekking agency*
- Manaslu Conservation Area entrance permit fee. *Nepal Tourist Board - Kathmandu.*
- Annapurna Conservation Area entrance permit fee.

The Special/Restricted Access Trekking permit must be obtained through your trekking agency. You can pay for and obtain the Manaslu and Annapurna Conservation Area entrance permit fees through the Nepal Tourism Board office in Kathmandu. However, since you're trekking with an agency, they will take care of it.

Please note, you don't need to obtain a TIMS card when you have to obtain a Special/Restricted Access Trekking Permit, which already tracks the number of trekkers an agency takes through the region.

For all the permits and park entrance fees, you'll need to submit four passport-sized photos to your trekking agency.

Arranging Transportation

Even though you arrive in Kathmandu to get ready for your trek, you won't actually begin your trek from there.

You'll have to take either a bus (local or tourist) or a private jeep from Kathmandu to the trek's starting point and then from the endpoint back to Kathmandu.

In this section, I'll outline the pros and cons of each type of transportation you can take. Sometimes, you'll won't have a lot of options depending on the town you find yourself in.

Local Bus *NO — too slow*

Taking the local is the cheapest option, but it's also the least comfy. The local bus is always crowded and drivers try to stick as many people on board as possible.

These buses are not maintained regularly and the drivers aren't the best. You can see them speed downhill on unpaved roads.

Here are the pros and cons of this transportation option:

- *Pros*
    - This type of transportation is cheap if you're a budget traveler.
    - You'll be immersed in the Nepali culture.
- *Cons*
    - It takes more than six hours to get to your destination.
    - Space is overcrowded.
    - No luggage internal compartment so the bigger bags are put on top of the bus.
    - Not the safest option for small groups or solo travelers.
    - Frequent stops to pick up travelers.

Tourist Bus   *possible if Ben doesn't want to hire a jeep!*

Compared to the local bus, this option is safer, more comfortable, and the buses are equipped with a luggage compartment. Taking the tourist bus is more expensive than the local one, but remember you're paying the extra amount to feel more relaxed and secure.

Just like the local bus, you can expect that the drivers will speed through the streets.

Here are the pros and cons of this transportation option:

- *Pros*
  - Cheap.
  - More spacious and more comfortable than local buses.
  - Luggage compartment equipped.
  - Buses leave on schedule or close to it.
  - Lunch stop.
- *Cons*
  - Leaves very early in the morning.
  - Takes six-seven hours to reach the destination.
  - Unsafe driver (safer compared to local buses).

Private Jeep

Hiring a private jeep to take you to your trekking start point is the most expensive of the options you can choose from. However, a jeep gives you more control over your drive. If you need to stop because you aren't feeling well or want to take a picture, you have the option.

You can also ask your driver to speed up or slow down if you're feeling nervous. And, you can be assured that your luggage will stay safe for the entire ride.

This option is great for groups since you can split the cost and it would be comparable to a bus ticket.

Here are the pros and cons of this transportation option:

- *Pros:*
  - Takes four-five hours to reach your destination.
  - Safe and secure luggage space.
  - More control over the ride.
  - Safest transportation option.
  - Comfortable seats.
- *Cons:*
  - Expensive if you're traveling alone.
  - May feel unsafe when a truck overtakes the car.

When I went on my trek, I took the local bus to and from Kathmandu. It is really crowded on the bus and it didn't have any air conditioning either.

I personally didn't have any problems with the space. I'm small and my legs didn't hit the seat in front of me when the bus drove over a bump or into a hole in the road.

Overall, I'm glad I took the local bus for my first time trekking in Nepal. However, if I go trekking again, I would pay the extra money to take a tourist bus or find enough trekking companions to hire a private jeep.

Storing Your Luggage

Storing your luggage while you're on the trek is a small detail you might overlook.

Remember, you won't take everything that packed for your trip, so you'll need a place to store those extra items.

You have two options:

- Store your luggage with your trekking agency.
- Store your luggage at the hostel or hotel you're staying at.

Both options offer to store your luggage for free in a secure room, where a limited number of staff members have access to.

If you're storing your things at your hostel or hotel, you'll need to reserve a bed for the night you return from your trek.

Remember to take most of your valuables with you and leave behind the clothes you won't need on the trek.

If you need to leave any valuables such as your laptop or other electronics, don't advertise its presence. Also, be aware that your bag may end up at the bottom of a pile of bags so pack your bag carefully.

Since I trekked with an agency, I left my bag in their secure room without any problems. The only valuable I left in my bag was a five-year-old tablet, which was neither stolen or damaged when I got my bag back.

Chapter 4: What to Expect on the Trek

One of the best things that helped me prepare was talking to other trekkers in my hostel room. These trekkers were either more experienced than me or had just returned from their trek.

I also had more than enough time to get ready for the trek. I walked around with different friends and learned what to buy, where to get it, and what price range to accept.

I was able to ask them what it was really like on the trails, at the tea houses, and tips they wished they knew before leaving.

I received advice from buying Snickers Bars as a snack (I didn't do it nor do I recommend it) to small things I would have forgotten such as toilet paper.

One roommate even gave me his hiking sticks since he didn't need them and couldn't fit them in his bag.

After receiving all the advice possible, it felt like I had fifty dress rehearsals before the big show! I felt more than prepared and was nervous I was going to forget something.

I hope this section will help you figure out the small details that will make your trek more enjoyable.

To start, I'll give you a general overview of the Manaslu Trek before going into a few details.

Overview of Manaslu

Before going into the particulars of the trek, here's a sample itinerary from the trekking agency I went with. Other agencies will have similar or even the same itinerary as the one below.

Sample Manaslu Trek Itinerary

Please note that all the altitudes listed and times are approximate and do not deviate that much from the actual. The altitudes listed are for the final resting point of the day.

If you'd like to know how long you trekked and how high you ascended, you can bring a watch that has those capabilities.

Day 1: Arrival in Kathmandu and transfer to hotel. You can come as early as you want before day 1.

Day 2: Drive to Aarughat (550 m) 7 hours

Day 3: Trek to Laphu Besi (884 m) 6 hours on the trails

Day 4: Trek to Khorla Bensi (970 m) 6 hours on the trails

Day 5: Trek to Jagat (1,450 m) 7 hours on the trails

Day 6: Trek to Dyang (1,850 m) 7 hours on the trails

Day 7: Trek to Namrung (2,500 m) 7 hours on the trails

Day 8: Trek to Shyala (3,400 m) 5 hours on the trails

Day 9: Trek to Sama Guan (3,500 m) 7 hours on the trails; visiting Pungyen Gompa

Day 10: Rest Day in Sama Guan (3,500 m) 3 hours on the trails; excursion to Manaslu Basecamp and Birenda Lake

Day 11: Trek to Sambdo (3,800 m) 4 hours on the trails

Day 12: Trek to Larkya Phedi/Darmasala (4,450 m) 4 hours on the trails

Day 13: Trek to Bhimthang (3,700 m) via Larkya La Pass (5,106 m) 9 hours on the trails

Day 14: Trek to Dharapani (1,960 m) 8 hours on the trails

Day 15: Drive to Besisahar (720 m) 5 hours

Day 16: Drive back to Kathmandu 6 hours

Day 17: Transfer to airport and departure to onward destination

On your trek, you can expect about 13 days of ascent, which includes a day for rest and acclimation. After climbing to and crossing the Larkya La Pass, you'll have 4 days of descent.

The first few days may be difficult depending on your physical fitness and outdoor adventure level. The Budhi Gandaki Gorge can be shockingly steep and narrow in some parts.

Keep in mind, the trail is new compared to Everest and Annapurna so its conditions aren't so tame or managed. No one on my trek was hurt during it, but don't trust every rock you see on the path.

The trail enters the Manaslu Conservation region right before you pass through Jagat. This is a significant mark on the Manaslu Circuit trek since you'll see a cultural shift from Nepali Hinduism to Tibetan Buddhism. For decades now, Tibetan refugees have fled and settled in this region for its remoteness and pureness.

In the Manaslu Conservation region, you'll see stone-roofed Buddhist villages such as Namrung, Lho, Samaguan, and Sambdo. All in the foreground of the of the magnificent Manaslu and Himalchuli Massif mountains.

Crossing the Larkya La Pass will be the hardest day of the trek and will test your willpower and resilience. You'll begin in snowy Larkya Phedi/Darmasala and finish in Bhimthang or a nearby village. On this day, expect to be on the trails for nearly 10 hours. The next day, you'll trek to Dharapini which is where the Annapurna Circuit Trek and Manaslu converge.

Daily Routine

Your daily routine on the trek is almost the same. Most days you'll be walking on the trails 6-8 hours with water breaks and a longer break for lunch.

A Typical Day on a Trek

You can expect to wake up anywhere between 6:00-6:30 AM and have breakfast half an hour later.

Before breakfast, you'll have time to do your personal routine, pack your bag, and prepare your day bag if you hired a porter.

Usually, you order your breakfast the night before so when you go into the dining hall your breakfast will be ready shortly. At breakfast, your guide will give you a brief overview of the day and tell you what to expect on the trails and things to look out for.

Around 7:30-8:00 AM you'll start hiking on the trails with your trekking companion(s), guide, and porter(s).

You could eat lunch anytime between 11am-2 PM. This is dependent on you and your trekking companion and if there's a village close by. For this reason, I highly recommend taking a small snack with you in case you get hungry before lunch or reaching your final destination.

In the lower altitudes, you usually reach your final destination around 4-5 PM. Before dinner, you can snack, rest, clean up, and prepare for the next day on the trails. In the higher altitudes, you usually reach your final destination around 2-3 PM.

Before dinner, I used the time to write in my journal, rest, and shower. In the higher altitudes, I saw more trekkers on the trails so I would journal in the dining room and talk to them.

Dinner is served around 6:00-6:30 depending on how many guests are at the tea house that night.

After dinner, your guide will talk about the next day and what time to wake up. Usually, trekkers will go to bed after dinner finishes. You'll be tired from the day and it will be dark enough where you'll start to feel drowsy anyway.

When you get a chance, look up at the sky before heading to your room for the night! You won't regret seeing a sky full of stars in a remote village in the mountains. Take it in because you'll have to come back to see it again!

On the Trails

While you're on the trails, you can see different plants, animals, and religious structures.

In the lower altitudes, you'll see a lot of donkeys carrying goods to the neighboring villages. The donkeys get the right of way on the trails so you'll need to move to the left. The donkeys won't stop for anyone so it's best to clear the path quickly!

Throughout the trek, you'll see various religious structures such as Stupas, Chortens or Maani Walls. People built Maani Walls with stone tablets with mantras written on them.

You'll notice the Maani Walls since they create a fork in the road. Always take the left road clockwise to show respect for the sacredness of the structure. Taking the left road is also for good luck!

In a similar situation, when you see spinning prayer wheels, always move and spin them clockwise.

In addition to walking on trails, you'll often come to big suspension bridges that are fun to walk across. Careful, when too many people get on it, it becomes hard to walk in a straight line!

When you walk through villages, a lot of children will come out and say "Namaste!" as you pass by. Wave and smile or say "Namaste!" back to them. Just don't give them any candies, treats, or money. It encourages begging and it doesn't help the kids in the long-run.

At the Tea Houses

Unless you're planning to camp, you'll be staying in a tea house every night on your trek.

Tea House Facilities

The tea houses are family run and have very minimal amenities than you might be used to. The rooms aren't big and don't have much insulation. In higher altitudes, you can request to have extra blankets for the night. The tea houses usually have plenty.

Typically, a double room has enough space for two beds and two duffel bags. There might be electricity running in the rooms, but it's often unreliable. If there isn't electricity, it can get quite dark towards the evening. If you want to read before bed, I'd recommend bringing a head torch with you.

The showers and toilets are down the hall from your room, which you share with the other trekkers for the night. Like your room, these aren't well insulated. If you end up making a trip there at night, be prepared to put on your warm gear and have some type of light with you.

The showers aren't the ones you're accustomed to. It's a bucket and a hose that runs cold water. If you really want, you can pay to have hot water, but you're usually just given a bucket of hot water. On my trek, I just bathed cold and in the higher altitudes, I used my trekking companion's baby wipes.

Everyone eats in the same dining hall and that's where it's the warmest! I spent more of my time there talking with other trekkers and journaling than my room-especially at higher altitudes. The electricity is usually more reliable in the dining area so I was able to journal or read there.

Spending Time at the Tea Houses

At the tea houses, you'll spend your time either in your room resting, talking in the dining area with other trekkers, or having some type of downtime. You can also use your downtime to walk around the village.

You'll be tired at the end of your days so you'll want to rest, reflect on your day, or talk to your fellow trekkers either in or out of your group!

Don't worry if you don't see many trekkers at the tea houses at the start of the trek. In the lower altitudes, everyone starts in a different spot or date. At some point, all the lower paths converge and you'll see the same people on the trails and the tea houses.

For me, I talked to my trekking companion at the beginning of the trek and my guide. When my trekking companion and I started seeing and meeting more people, we talked to others or even shared a meal together.

When I had altitude sickness, I did spend a little more time in my room resting right when we arrived at the tea houses. In the evening, I spent time talking with other trekkers I saw sitting in the dining hall.

Food and Water

Water

Remember, you'll need some way to purify your water on your trek! The tap water isn't safe to drink anywhere in Nepal.

Buy water purification tablets or a UV Water Purifier in Kathmandu before you embark. Both work the same except the tablets take 30 minutes to purify the water before you can drink it.

If you run out of purification tablets, you can buy more at a tea house along the way. However, be warned that the prices rise with the altitude! I highly recommend buying enough while you're in Kathmandu.

There are other drinking options if you need to drink something other than water. In the tea houses, you can buy hot chocolate, teas, hot lemon drinks, as well as soft drinks.

When I didn't drink water, I often drank milk tea or hot lemon tea, which helped keep myself warm in the higher altitudes.

Food

Tea houses along the trek offer similar menus to each other, some might offer different options depending on the season and region you're trekking in.

Overall, you'll be able to choose from a selection of pastas, tuna bakes, noodles, potatoes, eggs, dhal bat, bread, soups, fresh vegetables, and even desserts such as fresh fruits from the village.

If you're trekking without an agency, I recommend eating the dhal bat set. It's a traditional dish with white rice, lentil curry and local vegetables. This dish is filling and gives you energy for the next part of your trek! It's also the most cost effective since you can get free refills.

Another traditional dish I recommend trying is the momos, which are steamed or fried dumplings filled with meat and vegetables. They come with a Nepali dipping sauce, which is just delicious!

I tried the dahl bat on my trek and was not disappointed! I liked trying the traditional dishes since it helped me feel full for longer. I also ate dishes I was more familiar with, which were also good, but I wished I ate more traditional ones.

If you're worried about eating meat on the trek, I can assure you it's safe! I didn't very much meat while I was on the trek, but I didn't hear of anyone getting sick because of it.

Experiencing Nepali Culture

Nepali culture is a mix of different ethnic groups. You can experience anything from the remoteness life of the mountains and farms to the hustle and bustle of the big cities such as Kathmandu.

In the Manaslu region, you'll encounter the cultures and customs from the Tibeto-Burmans, or Mongoloids from the north, and the Indo-Aryans from the south. Both groups inherited customs from each other and have been further grown by the influence of the land, climate, and resources available.

On the trek, you'll primarily see Buddhist religious landmarks. Be on the look-out for Maani Walls, austere monasteries, chortens, and other religious landmarks.

The common courtesies, discussed in this section, are more flexible than they sound. However, if you're ever in doubt just ask or observe what the Nepali do.

If you follow these suggested guidelines, you'll feel more equipped to respect and experience Nepali culture.

Common Courtesies

When you're greeting someone either in Kathmandu or a village, say, "Namaste" with your palms held together in prayer. It's one of the most charming things you can do as a visitor. It shows that you respect the culture and are open to learning more.

Another delightful phrase to use is "dhanyabaad" which translates to "thank you" in English. This is normally used if someone goes out of their way to do something for you.

To come off as polite, give and receive anything with your right hand. Offer money, food, and gifts with both hands or with the right hand while the left touches the wrist. Doing so portrays respect.

Eating

In Nepal, once you've touched something with your lips, it's considered polluted; it's one of the underlying principles pertaining to eating.

To respect this custom, here are a few things you can do

- If you take a sip from someone else's water bottle, don't let your lips touch it.
- Don't eat off of someone's plate.
- Don't offer any food you've taken a bite of.
- Don't touch cooked food until you've paid for it.
- If you're eating with your hands, only use your right hand.

Temples

On the Manaslu trek, there are a couple opportunities for you to visit a temple or monastery.

When you're visiting a temple or monastery, please do the following to be respectful

- Take your shoes off before entering.
- Unless you have permission, don't take any photos.
- Leave a few rupees in the donation box if you can spare.
- Don't touch the shrines and offerings.

Meeting the Locals

Meeting the folk in the villages is the one of the best things you'll do on the trek! Kids will often approach you with smiles and enthusiasm as they shake your hand.

Some kids have become accustomed to receiving treats from trekkers and will run up and ask you for money, chocolate, or pens.

As I mentioned before, please do not give treats to the children. It encourages begging and doesn't add value to the local village economies.

I fully support and encourage you to interact and support the local villages but do not give away free things to the children.

Photo Taking

This topic is often up to debate wherever you travel.

In Nepal, you need to ask before taking someone else's picture. Most will say yes, especially children; however, it is common courtesy to ask.

It is frowned upon to not ask before taking a picture in a house or temple.

Chapter 5: Bumps on the Trails

There are common bumps you might experience on the trails such as Altitude Sickness, diarrhea, or loss of motivation.

First, I want to go over a few general safety precautions you can take on the trails before jumping into those specific bumps.

General Safety Tips

When you're trekking in Nepal, you'll be in remote areas in the mountains far away from any hospital or clinic.

These circumstances make it important to take the following precautions before and during your trek.

- Learn about Altitude Sickness (discussed in the next section). Take the acclimation days seriously, drink more water at higher altitudes, and listen to your body.

- Don't trek alone. If you're traveling solo, hire a guide or make a friend.

- Pay close attention to the weather conditions, especially on long pass days. Storms can come quickly and be deadly if you're not prepared.

- Make sure someone in your trekking group has a First Aid Kit.

- Give your trekking itinerary, trekking agency information, and important phone numbers to a trusted family member or friend while you're gone.

- When you see a line of donkeys or yaks, move to the side (usually the left) and let them pass before moving forward. These animals don't stop unless their leader commands them to and can be quite clumsy.

- Carry enough water on the trails with you and stay hydrated.

- Keep your eyes on the trail to avoid anything that could end your trek early.

- Be especially careful around landslide or avalanche areas.

- Crime is not common in Nepal, but that doesn't mean it couldn't happen to you. Keep all your valuables (passport, wallet, etc.) on you at all times or in your day bag.

Altitude Sickness and Diarrhea

When you hear stories about other people's trekking experiences, you seldom hear about them dealing with altitude sickness or diarrhea.

It makes sense, for your friends to talk only about the best parts of their trek. Especially, if you want to go on a trek yourself.

However, every great experience has some unappealing elements such as the ones I will discuss. It's important to know about it so you can deal with it properly and complete your trek!

Getting altitude sickness or diarrhea isn't a reason to turn back, it just means you have to take it slowly, listen to your body, and communicate with your guide.

Altitude Sickness

Altitude Sickness is common among trekkers, especially if you've never been at high altitudes before.

Altitude Sickness happens when the air pressure drops and less oxygen becomes available to you in higher altitudes.

If you experience Altitude Sickness, you'll start to notice symptoms around 3000-3500 meters.

These are the symptoms of Altitude Sickness

- Headaches
- Dizziness
- Fatigue and loss of energy
- Insomnia
- Shortness of breath

- Nausea
- Vomiting
- Loss of appetite

You'll lightly feel these types of symptoms within 12-24 hours of reaching a high altitude. As you acclimatize to the higher altitudes (during your acclimation day) these symptoms should subside.

If the symptoms don't subside, you'll need to take your high-altitude medication tablets. You'll take half a tablet in the morning and the other half in the evening.

The two types of altitude medication are

- *Ibuprofen*: Over the counter medication that can help with mild Altitude Sickness symptoms such as headaches or nausea.
- *Diamox (Acetazolamide):* Another over the counter medication that helps with more severe symptoms. This medication acts as a respiratory trainer and assists the body to process oxygen.

On my trek, I just took Diamox and Ibuprofen when I started experiencing Altitude Sickness Symptoms. At first, my guide had me take Ibuprofen, but when the symptoms didn't subside after a day, I used Diamox. I took the medication until my group started to descend.

Beware that Diamox makes your kidneys work twice as hard so you'll need to drink twice as much water at high altitudes. For me, instead of drinking 4 liters, I was drinking 8 liters!

Preventing Altitude Sickness

There are ways to prevent Altitude Sickness while on your trek. Of course, the best thing to do is walk slowly, but there are other pieces of advice. The following advice is what I received from fellow trekkers before and during my trek.

It's not purposed to replace what a medical professional would tell you. If you have additional concerns, please contact your doctor before embarking on your trek.

1. *Drink Water*
   At lower altitudes, it's recommended to drink at least 3-4 liters of water per day! This can include tea and soup at the tea houses.
   At higher altitudes, you need to drink twice as much water than at lower altitudes.
   It's easier at lower altitudes to drink 3-4 liters, but it becomes harder at higher altitudes since you're not sweating as much. Drink at every break so you ingest the needed amount of water.

2. *Avoid Leaps in Elevation*
   Once you reach a high altitude, avoid going up more than 1,500 meters in a day. Since you'll be with a guide through the Manaslu region, you'll be on an appropriate trekking schedule.

A common misconception is that physical fitness influences your ability to manage Altitude Sickness. As a result, many people who are "in shape" overlook acclimatization rules, trek too high too fast and show symptoms.

3. *Trek High, Sleep Low to Acclimatize*
   During your acclimation day, you'll trek and expose yourself to a higher altitude for a day. At night, you'll return to a lower altitude to rest and sleep.
   Doing this will help you acclimatize to the higher altitudes.

4. *Eat*
   On the trek, you'll be doing vigorous exercise for several hours a day. Fuel yourself properly with filling and healthy foods.
   Try local foods or fill yourself with healthy carbohydrates.
   If you buy snacks before the trek, try to find ones that will last throughout the journey. Nuts, muesli, peanut butter and the like are good choices.

5. *Pay Attention to Your Body*
   If you follow the advice above, you'll stay healthy throughout your trek! Having said that, everybody reacts differently to high altitudes so be in tune with your body.
   Every guided trek should have acclimatization or rest days built into its schedule.
   If you start to feel the symptoms of Altitude Sickness, tell your guide and he'll know how to help you from there! Keep your trekking

companions in the loop too so they can help you on the trails!

Diarrhea

Don't worry if you get diarrhea on your trek! It's the most common ailment that happens to trekkers. There are a number of reasons for diarrhea, but it's mainly believed that bacteria in non-purified water is the culprit.

Bacterial infection, although the main cause of diarrhea, it is not the only cause. Other causes include viruses, protozoa, some food and medicine, and possible allergies.

Usually, if you get diarrhea, you rest a couple days, replenish your fluids, and maybe see a doctor. In the mountains, you won't be able to see a doctor easily so self-diagnosis is vital.

If you do get diarrhea on your trek like I did on mine, here are a few tips to get you through it

- Rest
- Drink plenty of water
- Don't eat dairy products
- Avoid "hidden water" such as drinks with ice cubes
- Clean thoroughly all eating and cooking utensils
- Wash your hands after any contact with animals

- Dispose of any food that has been in contact with animals, including flies

Unlike when you get diarrhea in your hometown, you have limited food choice in the mountains. Ultimately, it will depend on how your stomach feels, but here are a few "safe" foods to try on your trek

- Plain rice
- Pasta
- Toast
- Crackers
- Bananas
- Vegetables

Fortunately, diarrhea is preventable on your trek just as if you were back home. However, due to the conditions, you'll be in, these following tips should be taken very seriously

- Purify your water.
- Wash your hands thoroughly after using the bathroom and before meals and even drinking.
- Don't eat raw foods. Your guide will make sure the cooks at the tea houses wash and boil the foods. For fruits, stick to ones you can peel such as bananas.
- Eat only sanitized dairy products.
- Clean thoroughly all eating and cooking utensils.
- Wash your hands after any contact with animals.
- Dispose of any food that has been in contact with animals, including flies.

When I had my run-in with diarrhea, I first told my guide. I took my stomach medicine, drank water at every stop we made. For meals, I ordered soup and just drank the broth. After doing those steps, it went away within a day.

Staying Motivated

On the trek, you might start to feel discouraged or less motivated for many reasons.

Perhaps, the Altitude Sickness symptoms were intense for you or the cold weather became really harsh.

When things start to get tough on the trek, just ask yourself why you wanted to make the journey.

Was it for the amazing views and getting out in nature?

Did you want to have an immersive cultural experience?

Or maybe it was a goal you wanted to achieve?

Use your personal reason to motivate yourself to push through even the toughest part of the trek.

When I was on my trek, the following tips help me push through my Altitude Sickness and complete the trek successfully.

Surround Yourself with People

You didn't come to trek alone so don't act as if you're an outcast or a loner.

Surround and talk with positive people!

While you might have a personal goal for embarking on a trek, this experience also lets you meet like-minded people.

When you socialize with other people, the less trouble you'll run into. Remember you want to be in a healthy environment, where everyone helps each other.

Make and Accept Mistakes

You can make a mistake as small as not packing your raincoat for the day, wearing the wrong pants, or even shoes.

Just be sure that you learn from the mistakes on your trek so everything else will go smoothly.

Think About the Big Picture

Don't be so concerned about the next village you need to trek to and the time it will take to get there.

Take the time to breathe and look at your surroundings. It's a not just the destination you're trekking for, it's the overall journey.

Some people make small goals for themselves to get through the tougher parts of the trek. It could be something small such as keeping an even trekking pace.

Take Pictures

Going on a trek is a once-in-a-lifetime opportunity! Take a few pictures to remember your time!

When you look back at the pictures, it will remind you about the things you couldn't capture with your camera. For example, a picture can remind you about how you felt, the cold spell that day, the conversation you had, and the one thing that made you feel happy.

Your pictures will serve as a memento for all the challenges you overcame to complete the trek. And, the people you met on the journey will make you feel empowered for years after the trek.

Chapter 6: Trekking Manaslu: A Day-by-Day Account

In this chapter, I want to share my personal account of my trek through the Manaslu Mountains. The details I have decided to share are less about the gear I used every day and more about the things I saw, the conversations I had, and some of the thoughts I had during the trek.

To give you a few background details, I went on my trek in October 2017 with a trekking agency. I arrived in Kathmandu a week and half before embarking on my trek. I hired a porter and a guide and had one trekking companion, whom I met the day I left, in my trekking group. For privacy reasons, I cannot say the name of my trekking companion, porter, or guide.

All the altitudes and destinations are the finals resting points of each day I was on the trails.

I decided to create this part of the book based on the itinerary my trekking agency gave me.

My hope that this part of the book will help you prepare for your Manaslu trek and give you a peek into the daily life of a trekker.

Day 1

For the first day of the trek, I had a meeting with the trekking agency and I picked up the duffel bag from them.

At the meeting, I met my guide, who talked about safety on the trails, Altitude Sickness, and what a typical day on the trails looks like. While I was at the meeting, I also dropped off my travel backpack in their secure room

After the meeting, I bought enough peanut-butter and muesli for 13 days on the trails and checked into the hotel that my trekking agency booked.

At the hotel, I double checked my gear list and packed it neatly into my duffel bag. I also prepared my day bag for tomorrow.

For reference, here is my final gear list:

- Warm hat for 5000 m altitude
- Warm jacket for 3000 m altitude
- Thermal gloves for 4000 m altitude and above
- Buff/Scarf
- Sunglasses
- Two 1 liter water bottle
- Towel
- Toilet paper
- Basic toiletries
- Rain jacket
- Rain pants
- Plastic bags for my phone and journal

- Diarrhea medications
- Altitude Sickness medication
- Water purification tablets
- Hand sanitizer
- One pair of shorts
- One pair of pants
- Thermal leggings
- Thermal base layer
- One shirt
- One tank top
- Two pairs of socks (one wool and the other hiking)

After packing my duffel bag, I went to dinner, and then to bed early since I needed to wake up at 5:00 to catch a bus.

Day 2

Final Destination: Aarughat

Final Altitude: 550 m

Today, I woke up and was ready to go at 5:00 AM.

In the lobby, I met my trekking companion, a woman in her late thirties from Finland!

Shortly after meeting my trekking companion, our guide and porters came to take us to the local bus station.

At the bus station, it was crowded, dusty, and a little chaotic. Unlike the buses I was accustomed to, the bus drivers try to fit as many people on board as possible! Since it was a local bus, there wasn't any air conditioning on the bus.

There were quite a few people sitting in the aisles. The luggage compartment is actually a rack on top of the bus. A few workers sit on top of the bus to ensure nothing falls off.

Riding on an 8-9-hour bus ride in Nepal is quite an experience.

As the bus drove out of Kathmandu, it was sitting in traffic for about an hour. When the bus stopped, kids tried to sell food or water to me through the bus windows.

Once out of the city, the bus drove through the bumpy, dusty, narrow winding roads through the countryside of Nepal! It was neat seeing the different landscapes and the rice fields.

At one point, there was so much dust on the road, that everyone had to close the windows, which intensified the hot and humidness.

After the bus ride, we arrived in a small village called Aarughat. It had a few guesthouses, a handful of family-owned shops and one trekking gear store.

I walked around the village before dinner with my trekking companion and got to know more about her.

She told me that she came to Nepal to do three treks in a row and she has also done treks in Peru!

It made me feel lucky I had a more experienced and encouraging trekking partner.

At dinner, we were given a summary of the next week and a half on the trails and what to expect as we trekked into higher altitudes.

Since this was my last night with the internet, I sent a quick note to my parents and close friends to say I will speak with them in a couple weeks!

Day 3

Final destination: Laphu Besi

Final altitude: 884 m

Total time on the trails: 6 hours

This morning, we woke up at 6:30, ate breakfast at 7, and started walking around 7:30.

It was really hot today on the trails especially when it became close to lunchtime. Most of the time I was thinking about how hot I felt and that I couldn't wait to take a cold shower at the end of the day.

The hardest part of the day for me was becoming accustomed to walking slowly.

When we entered a new village, many of the kids were excited to see new trekkers pass through. They would often run to the front door of their parent's house, wave, smile, and yell out "Namaste!".

Many of the villages look the same and can be small. The houses are made out of stone with a roof held down with rocks so it won't blow away when it's windy. Some houses have solar panels, internet, and sometimes a television antenna.

The paths fluctuated between narrow and wide depending on if we were walking into a village or between them.

At the tea house, I rested for the next day, took a shower, and wrote in my journal. I also tried talking with my trekking companion as well.

Since we had to get up at 6:30 the next morning, we went to bed early.

Day 4

Final destination: KhorlaBensi

Final altitude: 970 m

Total time on the trails: 6 hours

Today started just as the day before: wake up at 6:30, breakfast at 7:00, on the trails by 7:30.

On the trails, I crossed over several suspension bridges and walked on really narrow, rocky paths.

Since I was still in the lower altitudes, I was walking through very luscious green rain-forest-type plants and trees. I even heard a monkey in the distance!

Since we were walking along the Buri Gandaki River, we often were going up and down hills, which took us closer and further away from the river.

At one point, we were walking on the banks of the river bed! We needed to walk there instead of the path since the path was not maintained well.

On this day, I also saw a handful of waterfalls and several rice fields in the background.

At the tea house, I didn't see other trekkers so I followed the same routine I did last night. The tea house was close to the river and I could hear is roaring all night long! It was refreshing to fall asleep to the sounds of nature.

Day 5

Final destination: Jaghat

Final attitude: 1,450 m

Total time on the trails: 6.5 hours

Typical start to the morning and on the trails by 7:30.

Today, was the first time where I wasn't counting down the hours I had left on the trails and I really took in everything around me.

The trails were hilly today as they were yesterday, but unlike yesterday, there were "built-in" stairs so the inclines didn't seem so steep. Yesterday, we had a lot of inclines where we had to trek up a gravel hill.

Even though we didn't meet any new trekkers yet I was beginning to appreciate not having distractions. I was able to consider thoughtfully about what I really wanted and valued.

We arrived at our final destination for lunch instead of dinner which was nice for me. I had time to take a nap after lunch, hang up my trekking clothes, and have a moment to "breathe".

At dinner, we met two other trekkers from the United States! We swapped travel stories and what we thought about the trek so far.

Day 6

Final destination: Dyang

Final altitude: 1,850 m

Total time on the trails: 6.5 hours

Today, felt longer than any other day on the trails. My trekking companion and I decided not to have lunch on the trails since our guide said we'd arrive in Dyang in the early afternoon.

We actually arrived there around 3:00 which made the last part of our time on the trails a little frustrating.

On this part of the trails, the landscape started to change. We began to see less green and luscious plants and more burly-looking trees. We crossed even more suspension bridges and donkeys on the trail today. We had to move over for them numerous times.

Today, was also the first day I saw more people on trails and I had the option to talk to others! At the tea house, we met a big group of German trekkers, a couple from England, and saw the couple from the United States.

After I ate lunch and cleaned up, I sat in the dining area before dinner since it was warmer there and hoped I could meet and talk with other trekkers.

Day 7

Final destination: Namrung

Final altitude: 2,500 m

Total time on the trails: 7 hours

The trails were busy and crowded today because of the group of twenty Germans, especially in the morning since everyone left at the same time.

Like a cross-country or track race, the crowds of people began to thin out after the first hour and the trails became more pleasant for me.

What annoyed me was the number of people who took pictures of the Nepali kids without permission or gave them candy. I felt it was inappropriate and violated the culture.

The hills today were a mix between going straight up or curving hills so I didn't feel the elevation change as much.

I saw more cows than donkeys today, which made walking on the trails easier. I didn't have to move to the side for a line of donkeys.

Today was also the day, that my knees and balls of the feet started to feel sore from going up and down so many hills. When I told my guide, he let me use his tiger balm at the tea house that evening.

At the tea house, my trekking companion and I hung out in the dining area and journaled together. When she went to take a nap in our room, I began talking to the English couple I met last night until dinner time.

The English couple was well-traveled and each of them also traveled solo before meeting. They told me about traveling to South America together and again with their kids. They commended me for traveling the world alone and couldn't believe I wasn't done just yet!

After dinner, I was really happy that I was able to speak with other trekkers and this was the type of experience I was hoping to have.

Day 8

Final destination: Shayla

Final altitude: 3,400 m

Total time on the trails: 4.5 hours

The trails were steep today and took me and my trekking companion through chilly, shady forested areas. There weren't any winding hills with stone steps; it was all gravel steep inclines. It caused me to slip a few times, but I never fell!

Once we got to Shayla, I could finally see the Manaslu Mountains! It was pretty cool and I became really excited. I knew in a few days that I would pass through Larkya La Pass and be surrounded by the mountains' beauty!

After lunch, my guide took me and my trekking companion around the village and showed us the Buddhist temple. This village also has a helicopter landing in case someone needed to be airlifted.

Seeing the helicopter landing, reminded me to stay safe on the trails and emphasized how isolated I am from "normal" city services such as doctors.

I also began to feel less isolated the more I saw people on the trails. I can talk and receive advice from them. I haven't met anyone my age yet but I could meet someone before the trek ends.

Day 9

Final destination: Sauma Gaun

Final altitude: 3,500 m

Total time on the trails: 7 hours

On the way to Sauma Gaun, my guide took us to a mountainside monastery called Pungyen!

On the way to the monastery, we had to climb a very narrow rocky path, pass by a waterfall before we finally came to a flat part.

When we got to the monastery, I could see the north part of Manaslu and the Pungyen glacier! The monks were not at the monastery when we were there, but we saw the building where they sleep and the other part where they go to meditate.

Today, I started to feel as though I was getting altitude sickness, but once I drank more water my headache went away. My trekking companion advised me to tell our guide if my headache came back the next day.

At the tea house, I finally met someone around my age so I talked with her in the afternoon. In the evening, I played cards with her and her family before dinner.

Day 10

Final Destination: Sauma Gaun

Final altitude: 3,500 m

Total time on the trails: 3 hours

Today, was an acclimation day so instead of trekking to a different village, we took an excursion to Manaslu Base Camp and Birenda Lake. The Manaslu Base Camp is about 1,000 m above Sauma Gaun.

Due to my Altitude Sickness, I didn't quite make it to basecamp. My trekking companion did though! I had to turn back when my headache started to intensify.

What I really liked about the small excursion was seeing Birenda Lake. I could see the melting glacier fill it from a distance. I could see where the glacier used to be and the landscape it carved out.

I also heard several small avalanches and saw snow falling from the mountains.

It was there, I truly understood how unique my experience is out in the mountains. I realized that if I come back to this same spot in five years, the glacier will have receded more and the water level would have risen.

I thought about turning back since I felt so sick in the higher altitudes. My trekking companion reminded me that if I turn back, I'd have seven days on the trails whereas if I kept going I would have only four. She also said that we would climb up to 5,106 m over the course of three days so I should be able to handle it.

I decided to keep going and walk as slowly as I possibly could. I also planned to rest as soon as we got to the final destination of the day. I also had to start taking my altitude medications and eat foods with garlic in it to help my headaches until we went down in altitude.

Day 11

Final destination: Sambo

Final altitude: 3,800 m

Total time on the trails: 3 hours

Today, I walked really slowly and every time my guide asked if I needed a water break I said yes and even asked for additional ones.

It wasn't a steep day on the trails, we were walking in what seemed like valley since the trail was in the middle of two sloping mountains.

We had many hours of downtime at the tea house, so I used the time to rest, walk around the village with my trekking companion, and talk to all the trekkers I met on the trails.

Day 12

Final destination: Larkya Phedi (Darmasala)

Final Altitude: 4,450 m

Total time on the trails: 3 hours

Today we woke up at the same time as usual except it was snowing and foggy!

The snow eventually stopped during our time on the trails, but the fog did not let up until we reached our final destination.

The trails were not all the steep today except for one big hill. After, we walked through flatlands in the fog.

We didn't get a good view of the mountains today. I wasn't complaining since we had such great weather during the previous days of the trek. My guide said that the fog should clear up while we trek through the pass tomorrow.

At the final destination, we were put into tents to sleep! They were actually quite comfortable and warm.

I spent more time in the dining hall today than any other day since that's where everyone was hanging out. I met several new people and we compared our trekking experiences. We discussed our overall experience on the trails so far, how our guides helped us, and what we do back home.

The whole dining hall was full of excited and nervous energy since the next day, we'd all trek through the Larkya La Pass in route to Bhimthang.

It was supposed to be the hardest day on the trails but also the most fulfilling. We'd trek to our highest altitude (5106 m) and be surrounded completely by mountains and the people who helped make the journey more enjoyable.

After dinner, I went promptly to bed since we needed to wake up at 3:30 AM since it would take 9 hours to trek to Bhimthang.

Day 13

Final destination: Bhimthang

Final altitude: 3,700 m (via Larkya Pass 5,106 m)

Total time on the trails: 9 hours

This morning I woke up at 3:30 and got ready for the longest day on the trails. It was still dark and I was preparing my bag with the light on my phone.

I woke up with a small headache and a little trouble breathing. I knew it was going to be tough for me today on the trails, but I was determined.

After breakfast, I grabbed my day bag and decided to use my hiking sticks today upon my companion's suggestion.

We set out on the trails around 4:15 and it was still dark and a little windy. I couldn't see very well because I didn't have a head torch and my glasses kept on fogging up.

About twenty minutes into the trek, it became very hard for me to breathe, my headache intensified, and I felt nauseous. Following those symptoms, I ended up getting sick on the trails. After vomiting, my guide asked if I wanted to turn back and I said no. I would just take it very slow and need more help.

After that incident, everything went smoothly for the next hour and a half. It was quiet, cold, and just wonderful being out there with no distractions. My hands became so cold that I ended up not using my hiking sticks. I wanted to put my hands in my down jacket's pocket.

As the sun rose though, I did begin to feel warmer.

Before coming to a resting point, I did vomit again. At that point, my trekking companion's porter gave her bag to my porter and my guide took my day bag. My trekking companion's porter became my personal guide until we reached Larkya La Pass.

At the communal stop before the pass, many trekkers outside of my group checked-in with me! Apparently, a lot of people saw me get sick so they felt concerned whether or not I was going continue. The other trekkers commended me for pushing myself and gave me advice on how to continue safely.

After the communal stop, my trekking companion's porter and I went ahead of the rest of my group, so I was still without day bag, which had my water bottle and other daily necessities.

On our way to the pass, other trekkers and even guides continually checked-in with me and even offered their help!

When I finally saw the final hill to reach Larkya La Pass, I was so happy that afterward, my Altitude Sickness would fade away. I took a deep breath and slowly continue to hike up.

Once I got to the top, I saw everyone who I met over the last week. Many gave me a hug and congratulated me for making it through the toughest part of the trek. I felt proud for pushing my limits and overcoming the most challenging part of the trek.

I began to relax knowing everything will be easier going forward.

After catching my breath, I took a look around myself. I was completely surrounded by mountains for miles. It made me feel humbled and grateful for the unique opportunity and situation I found myself in.

I felt bonded with the other trekkers and those who helped me get to this point on the trek. Everyone was in a similar situation and was very willing to give their help or offer advice. It made me feel lucky and hope to give it back in some way!

The rest of the day went smoothly and was very long. It almost felt as though it was two days in one. After crossing the pass, all the trekkers began to spread out on the trails and I didn't see the same faces as frequently.

Once we got to our final destination, I was so happy to rest and journal.

At the tea house, I saw one of the guys I met yesterday. I was happy to chat with him after lunch. We compared our days on the trails and what we're looking forward to on the rest of the trek.

My Altitude Sickness did subside only to be replaced with diarrhea that night. I wished I could have stayed in the village an extra day to rest and replace my fluids, but since I had an itinerary to adhere to I had to trek the next day.

My guide told me to take medication for diarrhea, put a special powder in my drinking water, and only drink liquids at our meal stops.

Day 14

Final destination: Dharapani

Final altitude: 1,960 m

Total time on the trails: 8 hours

Today, was our last day on the trails since tomorrow we'd drive from Dharapani to Besisahar. The trails on the last leg, were too rocky and unpredictable for any trekker to safely get through.

The landscape I saw was similar if not the same to what I saw previously. While it was breathtakingly beautiful I didn't get as excited as I did the first time I saw it.

I thought about what I was going to do after the trek and began to appreciate the internet blackout. I was able to clear my mind, and really think about what I wanted and valued without the influence of other people.

I was looking forwarding to speaking with my parents and a few friends upon returning to Kathmandu. Before talking to my parents, I planned to contact people who could help decide what to do after the trek.

At the tea house, it was finally at a lower altitude where I wouldn't mind the cold showers! I didn't have to use my trekking companion's baby wipes for once and have a refreshing shower.

Day 15

Final destination: Besisahar

Final altitude: 720 m

Total time in the truck: 5 hours

To get to Besisahar, we had to take a local truck there. I was squeezed into a five-person truck with eight people including myself and the driver! The porters and guides sat in the truck's bed with my duffel bag. I kept my day bag in the truck's cab for security reasons.

The roads were really bumpy and often the driver's helper would have to get out of the car and move big rocks on the road just for us to get through.

Once we arrived at our destination, it felt like we were back in Kathmandu. The first thing I noticed that it was noisy and dusty just like the big city. I was starting to miss the quietness and solitude of the mountains.

Of course, I also was beginning to miss the people I was used to seeing every day on the trails or tea houses. It was weird that within a day, that community was gone.

Since I had internet again, I reached out to a few friends who could help me weigh my options going forward. I figured I could continue traveling, look for work in South East Asia, or return home.

I decided to wait until I got back to Kathmandu to check-in with my parents and my close friends.

Day 16

Final destination: Kathmandu

Final altitude: 59 m

Total time in the car: 6 hours

Today, we took a tourist bus back to Kathmandu so the ride was more comfortable than the one from the city. There was more leg room in between seats and the seats had more cushioning.

I slept most for the majority of the bus ride and talked to my trekking companion's porter whenever I woke up.

Once we arrived in Kathmandu, my trekking companion and I were transported to a hotel for the night.

We got dinner and then exchanged contact information to keep in touch!

After dinner, I finally gave my parents and close friend a call to let them know I completed my trek. I told them about my incredible journey through the Manaslu Mountains!

Chapter 7: End of Trek

For the final chapter of this short book, I will add a few final details about the trek and the takeaways.

Tipping Your Guide and Porter

Until recently, tipping was not an accepted practice in Nepal. Now, it is almost expected especially in the trekking industry.

The tip is dependent on how well you think your guide performed during your trek; however, 10% of your total trek's cost is average.

If you hired a porter, be sure that your guide splits the tip with him or give the tip directly to him.

Saying Good-Bye and Keeping in Touch

I encourage you to stay in touch with whomever you become close throughout your trek!

It could be your guide, porter, trekking companion, and even the other trekkers you met along the way.

When you return from your travels, you'll appreciate the occasional email you receive from a friend abroad.

You'll be surprised how delighted you'll feel having a piece of your travels with you at home.

Takeaway and Lessons Learned

When you are done with your trek, you'll be proud of yourself for accomplishing a goal! You can say proudly that you trekked up to 5,106 meters and back down and were surrounded by majestic mountains.

Beyond the pictures and stories, you'll tell your friends, there are lessons from the trek you'll take away from the trek.

Here are a few lessons I learned:

- *Short-Term v. Long-Term Strategies*
  You are probably familiar with short-term v. long-term strategies to reach your goals. However, going on a trek will push and test your physical and mental fitness and limits. After the trek, you'll have new limits to push and break.
  At some point, you get over the soreness and possible discomfort of trekking up and down hills for hours each day. After, you'll realize what you're capable of: more than you ever imagined.
  Take this lesson from the mountains to your "regular" life. Find barriers holding you back, break them to fulfill other life goals.

- *Values*
  While you're in the mountains, you'll probably won't be able to contact your close friends and family members. While in the beginning it might be hard or make you feel isolated, you'll push past it.
  When your head is clear and free from new distractions, you'll be able to focus on yourself. You might realize something you thought was valuable, no longer supports your goal.
  You have the time in the mountains to figure out what you value and how to achieve your new life goals.

- *Greater Self-Assurance and Confidence*
  Overall, the trek will make you question, doubt, and test you at times where you feel like you can't move forward.
  Yet, every step forward erases any self-doubt and builds more confidence and self-assurance that you can take with you even after the trek and leave Nepal.

Go on, put down the book!

It's time to create your once-in-a-lifetime experience in the Manaslu Mountains of Nepal!

About the Expert

Rebecca Friedberg graduated from The Ohio State University in 2017 where she pursed a degree in Classical Languages and a minor in Business Administration. After graduating, she traveled the world solo for six months.

Her travels took her to Spain, France, Germany, and Romania in Europe. In Asia, she traveled to Nepal, Thailand, Cambodia, and Vietnam.

Rebecca has wanted to trek after hearing her dad's world-traveling stories as a kid. She was delighted to have the chance to trek and create a unique experience for herself.

She wrote this guide to pass along advice she was given and help future trekkers.

This is Rebecca's first guide with HowExperts. She hopes to write other works in the future and travel.

HowExpert publishes quick 'how to' guides on all topics from A to Z by everyday experts. Visit HowExpert.com to learn more.

Recommended Resources

- HowExpert.com – Quick 'How To' Guides on All Topics from A to Z by Everyday Experts.
- HowExpert.com/free – Free HowExpert Email Newsletter.
- HowExpert.com/books – HowExpert Books
- HowExpert.com/courses – HowExpert Courses
- HowExpert.com/clothing – HowExpert Clothing
- HowExpert.com/membership – HowExpert Membership Site
- HowExpert.com/affiliates – HowExpert Affiliate Program
- HowExpert.com/writers – Write About Your #1 Passion/Knowledge/Expertise & Become a HowExpert Author.
- HowExpert.com/resources – Additional HowExpert Recommended Resources
- YouTube.com/HowExpert – Subscribe to HowExpert YouTube.
- Instagram.com/HowExpert – Follow HowExpert on Instagram.
- Facebook.com/HowExpert – Follow HowExpert on Facebook.

- Campylobacter - clarithromycin >> cyprofloxacin
- acetazolamide 125mg bd 24 hrs before rising to altitude & 250mg bd if AMS occurs
- Snacks for mid-morning + mid-afternoon

- rucksac
- head torch + spare battery + recharge cable
- Spare battery + recharge cable + usb/lightning cable
- sleeping bag + silk liner + inflatable pillow
- water filter
- 2x 1 litre sig bottles (1 clean / 1 dirty)
- alcohol gel for washing hands!
- small towel

- acetazolamide
- paracetamol

- waterproof jacket (breathable)
- waterproof trousers
- socks: 1 pair to wear / 1 pair spare
- walking trousers 1 pair
- Thermal trousers 1 pair
- Thermal top x 2
- gloves — wool
            \ silk liner
- wool hat / ? balaclava
- fleece
- ~~rugby~~ shirt [long sleeve sunscreen]
- sunglasses
- sun hat

Printed in Great Britain
by Amazon